"…and be subject to one another in the fear of Christ."

Eph. 5:21

Printed by CreateSpace, An Amazon.com Company

Available on Amazon.com and other online stores

(c) 2010, 2017 (Revised edition) W. David Thurman

All rights reserved. No part of this book may be reproduced in any form without the express written consent of the author.

THE CALL Logo by Mary Thurman

Author's Note: Most of the stories in this book are actual, true life events. A few of the stories are allegorical, although they may be based on real events. The names of persons described have been changed to protect their privacy.

Unless otherwise noted, all scripture quotations are from the New American Standard Bible.

Scripture quotations taken from the New American Standard Bible® (NASB),

Copyright © 1960, 1962, 1963, 1968, 1971, 1972, 1973,

1975, 1977, 1995 by The Lockman Foundation

Used by permission. www.Lockman.org

TABLE OF CONTENTS

PAGE

FOREWORD – "I HAVE A SOMEWHAT MATURE CONGREGATION…" 1

SECTION ONE – DEVELOPING A PLAN

1. COMMUNITY 7

2. OUR SOURCE 16

3. "I AND MY FATHER'S HOUSE HAVE SINNED!" 28

4. THE APPOINTED TIME 38

5. THE SURVEY 49

6. THE PLAN 62

7. TWO CULTURES 71

---RESOURCE #1: STEPS TO A PLAN 83

---RESOURCE #2: OUTREACH STRATEGIES, RESOURCES AND EVENTS 84

SECTION TWO – BODY WORK: EXECUTING THE PLAN

8. MOTIVATION 93

9. THE BUILDERS 102

10. ISOLATED	**114**
11. FORMING A BODY	**126**
12. FORMING A BODY (PART TWO)	**135**
13. CHANGE	**145**
14. STRUCTURAL INTEGRITY	**157**
15. "REMEMBER ME, O MY GOD!"	**167**
---RESOURCE #3: CORE VALUES	**178**
---RESOURCE #4: A MINISTRY FRAMEWORK	**179**
16. THE PALM OF HIS HAND	**182**
THE LAST WORD	**192**

FOREWORD – "I HAVE A SOMEWHAT MATURE CONGREGATION..."

My friend and I had lunch together with my friend's pastor. The pastor was young, bright, well read and well-spoken. We discussed ongoing ministries, and then we talked about our respective churches.

The pastor reflected. "I have a somewhat..." The pastor slowed down the pace of the sentence at the word "somewhat" as if he were measuring it carefully. "I have a som-m-mewhat mature congregation" he said.

The sentence, and its delivery, struck me as unusual. "What do you mean by 'somewhat mature?'" I asked.

"I'm really not sure." The pastor paused. "We have a number of older people in our congregation. I guess I would describe them as 'experienced Christians.' They have been churchgoing Christians for a long time."

"Would you say they are fruitful Christians?" I asked.

The pastor paused again. "I had not really thought of it that way" he replied.

I explained. "The reason I ask about 'fruitful Christians' is that fruitfulness is a scriptural mark of maturity. Jesus uses so many agricultural analogies - the parable of the sower...the parable of the fig tree. They all point toward fruitfulness. Fruitfulness is the mark of maturity for one planted in the kingdom of God. It's John 15:8: 'By this is my Father glorified, that you bear much fruit, and so prove to be My disciples.'"

My friend interjected. "You know, in our church I think we've only had 1 or 2 conversions in the last 5 years."

"And the conversions are extremely important" I added. "But conversions are only a part of fruitfulness."

We discussed the pastor's church. "I have such a diverse congregation" the pastor said. He went on to describe different "camps" within his body. There were the "traditionalists" - people who liked the present order of worship (liturgy) and did not want to change the church service or the way the church functioned. Then there were the "orthodox." The orthodox wanted to return to a more formal church service and tended to be more dogmatic than the traditionalists. Finally, there were the "charismatics." The

charismatics desired more freedom and wanted to relax the order of worship in order to facilitate the "move of the spirit."

The pastor thought for a minute, and then shook his head. "I don't know how such a diverse group of people ever got into the same church."

My friend shared that he was serving on the "vision committee" for the church. This committee had been seeking the Lord for vision for that church. "Is there any way that such diverse people will agree on a common vision for a body?"

"Isn't that the pressing question?" I asked.

And that is a pressing question. Does God just call individuals to a work, or does He call groups of people – even churches – to a common work?

God does call groups of His people to a mutual goal... a common vision. Scripture is full of examples where God instructed a group of people to fulfill a specific vision or call. The key lies in identifying that vision or call, and then committing to it corporately and pursuing it.

And that pastor's congregation of diversity, why are they placed together in the same body? The members can focus on their differences and divide. Or they can realize that diverse gifts are necessary to fulfill a corporate call. They can coordinate their diversity to fulfill God's call for them and be fruitful as a body.

In our first book, THE CALL (Book One – Functional), we discussed specific, functional steps that an individual can take to become fruitful - to make disciples in the kingdom of God. In the second book, THE CALL (Book Two – Foundational), we explored the concept of "call" in more detail, and discussed the gifts that are needed to fulfill that call. We explained how the gifts operate on an individual basis. We then expanded the scope and proposed ways that those same gifts work cooperatively on a corporate basis.

This book is more challenging. This book describes a corporate call for a collection of believers...a "church." The variety of calls that the Lord can give to an individual or to a group are limited only by the breadth, height, depth and scope of God Almighty Himself. God alone directs. My encouragement, though, is to consider the corporate call that is described in this book and to ask Him if this call, or a variation of it, might be the direction that the Lord has for your body.

This book has two sections. In the first section, "Developing a Plan," we discuss steps to discern and formulate a plan to reach a community and its people. In the second section, "Body Work - Executing the Plan," we explore principles needed to implement and fulfill the plan that God gives.

This book draws lessons and instruction from the Book of Nehemiah. The Book of Nehemiah describes a call to a community of believers in a very difficult time, and how that community functioned to fulfill that call. I encourage you to read the Book of Nehemiah before you read this book. Then as you read each lesson in this book, go back and read the chapter of Nehemiah referenced in each lesson.

The principles expounded in the first two books, THE CALL (Book One – Functional) and THE CALL (Book Two – Foundational), are helpful for a body to fulfill the corporate call in this third book. THE CALL series was written progressively. The first two books will assist you in a deeper understanding of this third book, and they provide a foundation for the work described here.

How can a body become fruitful with lasting impact?

By changing the community around it.

SECTION ONE:
DEVELOPING A PLAN

LESSON ONE - COMMUNITY

"The wall of Jerusalem is broken down and its gates are burned with fire..." Neh. 1:3

Dewey struggled at Boyz Club. Boyz Club had a number of dysfunctional members. But it wasn't other boys at Boyz Club that made Dewey struggle. Dewey struggled at Boyz Club because Dewey struggled at life.

Dewey came from the backwoods of Kentucky. He was a raw-boned country boy who spoke with a heavy mountain twang. Dewey kind of stood out at Boyz Club. Boyz Club had broad diversity with many Asians, Africans, and Arabs. But Boyz Club did not have many rednecks.

Dewey struggled for a couple of other reasons. Dewey was raised in deep poverty. His parents did not want to live in the crowded inner city, but their destitution did not leave them much choice. Dewey's family lived in a roach-infested apartment; then in an old extended stay hotel; and then with his grandparents. They stayed just one step ahead of the rent collector.

One weekend, Dewey attended a soccer camp with other Boyz Club members. After the camp, Dewey hitched a ride home with Patrick, a Boyz Club leader. When they arrived at Dewey's place, Dewey and Patrick were surprised to learn that the premises were vacant. Dewey's family had moved over the weekend. Dewey did not know they were moving.

Dewey had a temper. He didn't like being teased about his country accent or his tattered clothes. He riled easily and fought eagerly. One school year, Dewey received suspensions totaling 36 days for fighting. He failed school that year. He failed 9th grade four times. Dewey was an easy target.

One reason that Dewey was an easy target was his reputation for tall tales. Dewey told wildly unbelievable stories about his exploits and then defended them as the gospel truth. The other guys teased him about it mercilessly. On one Boyz Club retreat, I had Dewey, Jorge and Tywan in the car. We talked about the places we had visited.

"Last year," Dewey boasted "I went to Europe for six months."

Jorge snorted. "Dewey, you did NOT go to Europe last year."

"I did too!" Dewey fired back. "I went there …on business."

Jorge shook his head disdainfully. "Alright, Dewey, where did you go in Europe?"

"I went to London."

"Sure you did. And what did you see there?"

"I saw the Eiffel Tower!"

Jorge snorted again. "You didn't see any Eiffel Tower!"

"Dewey," I interjected, "the Eiffel Tower is in France." The other guys in the car chortled.

Dewey fired back. "Yeah, well I went to France too!"

"Okay hot shot!" tested Jorge. "How did you get from London to France?"

"I drove a car!"

"Across the English Channel?!!"

"They had a big bridge!"

The guys in the car laughed again, led by Jorge. And so it went. The deeper Dewey waded into fantasy, the harder the guys rode him. And the madder he got. But that did not keep Dewey from telling the next whopper.

Dewey never backed off a story. He always defended his tales loudly and seriously. Dewey jumped from explanation to excuse – even if the present excuse completely contradicted the prior minute's explanation. Dewey acted as if he genuinely believed his yarns.

I often wondered why Dewey came to Boyz Club. He didn't play sports well during the recreation time. He was generally mocked for who he was, for what he looked like and for what he said. Dewey argued with the other guys and got into fights. He almost never participated in Bible study discussions.

One day at Boyz Club, though, Dewey seemed subdued. He didn't come in bragging about his latest escapade. He didn't talk during the recreational time or the meeting. Something was obviously bothering him.

At prayer time, I asked for prayer requests. Dewey slowly raised his hand. When I recognized him, Dewey's eyes misted and he looked down at the floor.

"It's my granddaddy!" Dewey said. Dewey often talked about his grandfather. Dewey had lived with his grandparents off and on during his young life. I knew his grandfather meant a lot to him.

"My granddaddy…" Dewey choked and fought back tears. "My granddaddy is bad sick and they say he may not make it." Dewey continued looking down. A couple of large tears hit the floor at Dewey's feet. Dewey wiped his eyes with his sleeve. No one doubted him now.

Then a hand appeared on Dewey's shoulder. It was Jorge. "Dewey, it's going to be okay" Jorge said. Slowly the guys gathered around Dewey and put their hands on him. Then we prayed for Dewey and for his grandfather as Dewey sobbed.

For years after that, Dewey came to Boyz Club. In fact, long after Dewey was too old for Boyz Club, he still came – hanging around the edges and helping where he could. What I realized is that Dewey did not have many friends, and he certainly did not have many places to "hang his hat."

But at Boyz Club, Dewey found something special. He found something both precious and necessary. Yes, the guys still laughed at Dewey and teased him. But Dewey had found a place where people cared for him. He found a place to belong.

Dewey had found community.

Community is a place of connection. It is the place that we rub elbows and bump knees with the same people that we hug. In community, you receive mercy for a need from the same person with whom you argued last month. As Dewey discovered, in community no person is immune from a taunt, but only because everyone is deeply known. In community, strengths are displayed in the same way that weaknesses are exposed.

Perhaps most importantly, community is a place of influence. By entering and engaging in community, a person acquires the standing to share and to be an example.

> PRINCIPLE: Community is the place of influence.

Jesus understood this fact. When He sent His disciples on a mission to preach, He sent them to enter the cities and villages of Israel. Lk. 9:6; 10:1. His instructions focused on presentation of the gospel in word and in deed to each community. "Preach...heal...raise...cleanse...cast out...give..." Mt. 10:7-8. The purpose of the disciples' mission was to bring the Kingdom of God to the hearts and life of the community. "And as you go, preach, saying, 'The Kingdom of heaven is at hand.'" Mt. 10:7. "[A]nd say to them, 'The Kingdom of God has come near to you.'" Lk. 10:9.

The mission of the disciples concerned authority. Either the community submitted to the authority of the Lord, or it rejected His authority. Each community accepted the truth of the Gospel, or the community denied that truth. As a result, peace and wholeness covered that place, or it was "returned to sender." The authority of the Kingdom rested in that place, or a curse of judgement plagued it. Lk. 10:8-15.

> PRINCIPLE: The purpose of the disciples' mission was to establish God's authority in a community.

THE SYMBOL OF AUTHORITY

Imagine the largest manmade structure that you can think of. Fix it in your mind.

Now, how big is it? How much square footage does it cover? Is it a skyscraper? Maybe a cathedral in Europe? How many people can it hold? What is its purpose?

The largest manmade structure in the world is not measured in terms of square feet. Most people describe it in terms of miles...thousands of miles to be exact. The largest structure in the world is the Great Wall of China. According to Wikipedia, the Great Wall of China with all its branches, extends 5,500.3 miles. It is the longest fortified line in the world. The legend is that the Great Wall of China is the only manmade structure that can be seen with the naked eye from space.

Now it happened in the month Chislev, in the twentieth year, while I was in Susa the capitol, that Hanani, one of my brothers, and some men from Judah came; and I asked them concerning the Jews who had escaped and had survived the captivity, and about Jerusalem. And they said to me, "The remnant there in the province who survived the captivity are in great distress and reproach, and the wall of Jerusalem is broken down and its gates are burned with fire." Now it came about when I heard these words, I sat down and wept and mourned for days; and I was fasting and praying before the God of heaven. Neh. 1:1b-4.

The Book of Nehemiah is instructive for us. The work which it describes, and the challenges Nehemiah faced, help us understand how to change a community. The Book of Nehemiah begins with a report about the city of Jerusalem and its condition. The city's walls and gates are broken, and its people are in reproach. That report sends Nehemiah into mourning.

In the days of the emperors of China, as well as in the days of Nehemiah, a wall had a purpose. To citizens inside a wall, the wall meant safety, protection and security. For the ruler(s) of a walled city, the wall signified dominion and power within the community. To enemies outside of a wall, a wall presented an imposing obstacle that was difficult to overcome.

The most feared enemy the Romans faced was Hannibal of Carthage. With his cavalry of elephants, Hannibal invaded Italy. Despite overwhelming odds, Hannibal used his strategic genius to defeat massive Roman armies in battle after battle. Many historians regard Hannibal as the greatest military tactician ever.

But Hannibal never conquered the city of Rome. According to legend, Hannibal approached the city in 211 B.C. after numerous crushing victories. When he arrived, however, Hannibal saw the formidable Servian Wall which protected Rome. He realized that he did not have the men or material necessary to overcome it. Hannibal personally approached the wall and symbolically threw a spear at the city. But he could only manage this famous token of defiance.

Hannibal then broke camp, turned, and retreated with his army to eventual defeat.

A large and impenetrable wall is a symbol of strength and authority. The wall establishes an environment of peace and security for those persons within its protection. Its enemies are prevented from infiltrating that environment and inflicting harm.

> PRINCIPLE: A wall is a symbol of strength and authority.

That is why Nehemiah felt such dismay upon hearing the news that the walls of Jerusalem were broken down. Any city without a fortified wall was a community in distress. That community was exposed and subjected to the cruel designs of its enemies.

The broken walls told the spiritual state of Jerusalem. Years before, the king of Judah had done "evil in the sight of the Lord His God." II Chr. 36:12. "Furthermore, all the officials of the priests and the people were very unfaithful following all the abominations of the nations; and they defiled the house of the Lord which He had sanctified in Jerusalem." II Chr. 36:14. Therefore God "brought up against them the king of the Chaldeans." The Chaldeans "burned the house of God, and broke down the wall of Jerusalem and burned all its fortified buildings with fire, and destroyed all its valuable articles." II Chr. 36:17-19. The reproach of the community was not only physical, it was spiritual. The broken walls bore witness to the rejection by the people of Jerusalem of the Lord's authority in their lives and in their city.

> PRINCIPLE: To Nehemiah, the broken walls of Jerusalem symbolized its spiritual desolation.

The city needed restoration.

COMMUNITIES TODAY

I have driven down Westward Drive hundreds of times. Westward Drive is a major thoroughfare in my city that is near my suburban home. On Westward Drive are businesses, gas stations, houses, a Wal-mart, and a sign at a driveway that says "The Grove." After fifteen years I had noticed most of the businesses and houses. I had filled up at the gas stations and shopped at the Wal-mart. But I had never noticed the sign that says "The Grove."

One day, a young man came to Boyz Club. At the end of the Boyz Club meeting, he asked me for a ride home.

"Where do you live?" I asked. This question was always relevant when providing transportation.

"The Grove" he replied.

"Where is that?" I asked.

"Westward Drive."

"Westward Drive?" I asked perplexed. "Where on Westward Drive?" His answer surprised me, because he described a location less than a mile from my house. But I had never noticed it. I agreed to give him a ride home.

When I turned onto the driveway at the sign for The Grove, I wasn't prepared for what I saw. The small driveway off of Westward Drive opened into a crowded community of hundreds of apartments. Thousands of people lived there. Scores of poorly dressed young people milled about aimlessly, many of them barefoot and shirtless. A few older cars and trucks sat in front of the buildings. Some of them were on cinder blocks or missing windshields. Most had splotches of rust on them. In the middle of the complex was a small open area in which a few young men were kicking a ball. The area was brown with only a few patches of grass on the side. It was littered with glass and trash. This community was obviously very poor.

I had no idea. But today, the work of the Lord is being done inside the Grove.

My city has pockets of poverty. Downtown is governed by the kings of power and the princes of commerce. It is dominated by skyscrapers, multi-story condominiums, and tight security. Branching off of downtown, affluent and suburban neighborhoods adorn tree-lined boulevards. Lush parks, large stores and huge churches define these communities.

Interspersed between these upscale districts are pockets of poverty. These are crowded complexes where thousands of people live on an acre or two of land. They are connected to the city by narrow driveways rarely used by outsiders except for utility trucks, waste management vehicles and police cruisers.

These areas are not just pockets of poverty. These areas are *isolated* pockets of poverty. They are "eye-sored" - fenced off and walled off so that they are out of sight. Our institutions of prestige are busy protecting the rest of us from the sights, sounds and smells of poverty. Isolation is the best protection. So the driveway to Wal-mart is larger and far better marked than the driveway to The Grove. Wal-mart is wide open. The Grove is hidden. The Grove is there though. It is probably near your house. All you have to do is to look for it.

Here is the bottom line: Our communities today are broken just like the walls of Jerusalem.

But our reproach is not just the brokenness in our midst. Our reproach is our outlook. We disdain the poor around us so we can focus on our own ostentatious luxury. Instead of restoring our poor, we hide them so we can ignore them. Our institutions spend billions promoting entertainment, self-fulfillment and gratification. Our culture honors selfish excess. But we closet the poor.

Our walls are broken down. We need restoration.

My friend, Gretel, is a social worker. We were walking back from court one day and Gretel said, "Can you believe it, David? The Department of Social Services made its own social worker go through sensitivity training."

"What happened?" I asked.

"Some foreign woman came into the Department building. She needed to use the bathroom but she didn't know what the facilities were for. When the social worker walked into the bathroom, the woman was crouched down and peeing on the floor. The social worker tried to stop her, but that foreign woman couldn't speak any English. So the social worker yelled at her. So her supervisor made the social worker go through sensitivity training. Unbelievable!"

"Gretel," I said "the foreign lady was probably doing what they did in her native country."

"Yeah, but the *social worker* isn't the one peeing on the floor. That's disgusting!"

I paused for a moment. "Gretel, don't you see? That is how we all appear to Jesus. What we think, what we say, the things that we do...it's disgusting to Jesus. To Him, we are peeing on the floor whenever He walks into the room.

"But He doesn't yell at us or scold us. Instead He compassionately loves us and cares for us. He understands that we are in need of restoration."

Our communities need restoration. Just as Nehemiah saw the need for a wall to establish God's rule in Jerusalem, we need the Lord's authority and peace in the communities near us and around us. But how do we begin the process of restoration?

MEDITATION: "They push the needy aside from the road; the poor of the land are made to hide themselves altogether." Job 24:4.

1. Have you ever been a part of a community?

2. What was the community like?

3. Do you know of any "pockets of poverty" in your city?

4. What are the keys to restoration in those places?

5. What does security for a community mean to you?

REVIEW:
1. Community is the place of influence.
2. The purpose of the disciple's mission was to establish God's authority in a community.
3. A wall is a symbol of strength and authority.
4. To Nehemiah, the broken walls of Jerusalem symbolized its spiritual desolation.
5. Our communities today are broken just like the walls of Jerusalem.
6. Our communities need restoration.

RELATIONSHIP >

LESSON TWO – OUR SOURCE

On June 21, 2009, the first day of summer, a tree fell at our Church.

THE TREE

At 1:30 PM on Sunday, June 21, 2009, I was returning from a Boyz Club weekend retreat. While parking a van in the church parking lot, I was surprised to see a large tree lying across the street in front of the church. My first thought was "That is strange. I don't remember any wind."

I impulsively looked at the sky. Usually trees fall during storms, blown down by a strong wind. But I hadn't seen any evidence of storms or wind on the drive back to the city. The sky was bright blue.

I walked down the street to investigate. As I got a better look at the tree, I grew more perplexed. There was no "root ball." I have spent a lot of time in the woods, and I have seen thousands of fallen trees. Almost always, the force of a falling tree rips out its roots. But this tree did not have a root ball.

Why did the tree fall? Before answering this question, I want to describe the tree. The tree was a huge tulip poplar. On the day before the tree fell, it was expansive and flourishing. The tree had large branches covered with green leaves. A few weeks before, an arborist had inspected the trees at the church, and pronounced this poplar sound. When the city workers cut the tree in six-foot sections the day after it fell, the wood in each cut was solid. The core of the trunk was not hollow or decayed. In all respects, the tree appeared healthy. Any person looking at the tree on the day before it fell would have said "My! What a beautiful, thriving tree!"

But on Sunday, that tree fell. As I approached the base of the fallen tree, I noticed that the trunk was black on the end. The very bottom of the tree - the place where the trunk connects to its roots - was rotten. Because of this decay, the tree had separated from its roots - its anchor, and simply fallen over. In fact, there was a large hole in the ground left by the fallen base.

THE SOURCE

The roots of a tree are its life source. The roots provide water and nourishment from the soil for the whole tree. This tulip poplar thrived in every respect - except it lost its connection to its source. Rot and decay at its base had strangled its life flow.

As I looked at the tree, it reminded me of a body - a body like our church. To thrive, the body must maintain its life connection with the Lord - its Source. Ephesians 3 came to mind:

For this reason I bow my knees before the Father, from whom every family in heaven and on earth derives its name, that He would grant you, according to the riches of His glory, to be strengthened with power through His Spirit in the inner man, so that Christ may dwell in your hearts through faith; and that you, *being rooted and grounded in love,* may be able to comprehend with all the saints what is the breadth and length and height and depth, and to know the love of Christ which surpasses knowledge, that you may be filled up to all the fullness of God. Eph. 3:14-19.

"Rooted and grounded in love." Love - the greatest commandments. To love the Lord your God with all your heart, soul, strength and mind. And to love your neighbor as yourself. Lk. 10:27. This love flows from connection with the Source.

But the Ephesian church - the church to whom Paul wrote this epistle...the church with which Paul spent years in ministry - does not exist anymore. Ephesus is now an archaeological ruin. It is a historical curiosity visited by thousands of tourists. I thought of the letter to the Ephesian church in Revelation:

I know your deeds and your toil and perseverance, and that you cannot tolerate evil men, and you put to the test those who call themselves apostles, and they are not, and you found them to be false; and you have perseverance and have endured for My name's sake, and have not grown weary. But I have this against you, that you have left your first love. Rev. 2:2-4.

The Ephesian church had labored in deeds and toil. It had persevered and maintained doctrinal purity. But it had lost its connection. It had forsaken its love. Then the next phrase struck me:

Therefore remember from where you have fallen, and repent and do the deeds you did at first; or else I am coming to you and will remove your lampstand out of its place - unless you repent. Rev. 2:5.

THE IMPACT

What was the impact of the fallen tree? The tree fell across the street in front of the church and knocked down numerous overhead wires. For a few days, our church lost its telephone and its internet - its ability to communicate. It also lost its electricity – its power.

But the fallen tree did not impact just our church. It fell across the street and damaged a neighbor's truck. The neighbor's grandchildren were visiting him, and one grandchild's tricycle was crushed. Thankfully, the grandchildren had slept late and no one was playing in the neighbor's front yard when the tree fell.

The fallen tree impacted more people than just the neighbor across the street. The power lines that fell were located on a trunk line. Hundreds of homes in the area were without power. The outage was so extensive that an item about it appeared on the evening news.

I looked and saw people coming out of their houses along the street. The first day of summer was extremely hot. I felt bad for our neighbors that would have to suffer in the heat for hours or maybe even days without air conditioning because our tree fell. Our church administrator felt the same sympathy. He wanted to help them. His statement was telling. "I would invite them to come stay inside the church, but it wouldn't do any good because *we don't have any power either.*"

AN APPLICATION

The day the tree fell - June 21, 2009 - was an important day at our church. It was a day that the church was scheduled to vote on the annual budget for the body.

Our budget is an indicator of our heart. If a person wants to know how a church feels about missions, look at the budget. If a person wants to know how a church feels about Christian education, look at the budget. Worship, pastoral ministry, the neighborhood, the poor, training - the depth of real concern is shown by the budget. Jesus put it succinctly: "Where your treasure is, there will your heart be also." Mt. 6:21. Our budget discloses our love. It reveals how intimately we are connected to the Source.

The application is simple. If our budget is motivated by love for God with all our heart, soul, strength and mind, and by love for our neighbor as ourselves, our body will thrive.

If our budget is not motivated by love for God with all our heart, soul, strength and mind, and not by love for our neighbor as ourselves, but by a different motivation, our body will fall.

It is all about our Source and our connection to it.

"Now it came about when I heard these words, I sat down and wept and mourned for days; and I was fasting and praying before the God of heaven." Neh. 1:4.

CONNECTION

This is the foundation for ministry: Intimacy ... A strong and close relationship ... A deep and abiding Presence ... The hand of the Lord on our life and activity. It is all about connection.

Mark,

Thank you for the time together at lunch yesterday.

Your question about balance in your life was profound – how to balance work, family and ministry. It is something that I have struggled with for years, and I continue to battle. So much of it seems to boil down to a discernment of what expectations arise from a worldly culture, and what actually arises from the culture of God's kingdom. (I still am shocked by the impact of this discernment on the lifestyle of Jesus.)

Maybe you and I will have the opportunity to explore this issue on a more personal level later. I will share with you a couple of things that I did with my children (to whom I am strongly bonded emotionally):

When my children were young, I read to them almost every night. Our routine was to eat supper together, and then I took the children and read to them storybooks, Bible stories, etc. We had a lot of playtime as well, but the reading was a great time to bond and interact, and an educational boost.

After my children grew old enough to read on their own (which they continued to do), I began taking walks with them every night when I came home. We sometimes went and played games or hit a playground, or we just walked. I still do this with my girls who are at home (ages 17 and 14). It is a chance to "debrief" and to listen, and to guide and advise. For me, walking with my children is a highlight of the day, and during the day, the prospect of walking with my children is an uplifting thought. It encourages me.

Reading and walking are great activities, but there are many ways to enhance relationship. I guess I am saying that I tried to find something to do together with my children to enhance relationship that I could incorporate as a part of daily routine. It was intentional, but it became routine.

Keep up the good work,

David

We understand the necessity for maintaining connection. Without connection, our families dissolve. Without connection, our friendships fade. Without connection, our businesses fail. Yet we often expect resource from God without maintaining our connection to Him.

Nehemiah understood about connection. The king of Babylon was the most powerful man on earth. To his subjects, the king was a god. And Nehemiah saw the king of Babylon on a daily basis. In fact, Nehemiah not only saw him, he was the king's close adviser and confidant. He was the king's cupbearer. Nehemiah had connection.

Such connection is normally announced as part of introduction. "Hi, my name is Nehemiah, and I am the king's cupbearer." But that is not how Nehemiah begins his book. The first chapter of Nehemiah describes the desolate state of Jerusalem (1:1-3), and then abides in prayer (1:4-11a).

Finally, at the end of the first chapter after his extended prayer and intercession, Nehemiah adds "Now I was the cupbearer to the king." Neh. 1:11b. To Nehemiah, his high office was an afterthought. Nehemiah understood that God was his Source.

The source is necessary for function. If a lamp is not plugged into that little electrical outlet in the wall which is its source of power, we remain in darkness. If the finest fire engine in the world is not connected to the fire hydrant which is its source of water, the house will burn down. Our God is the Source of light, of power, of sustenance, of design, of joy, and of life itself. We must maintain connection to Him. "I am the vine, you are the branches; he who abides in Me and I in him, he bears much fruit, for apart from Me, you can do nothing." Jn. 15:5. Ongoing connection is necessary. And Nehemiah understood that fact. So he began his story with prayer, not his position.

> PRINCIPLE: We need God's continuous presence in our lives in order to do God's work.

This is the most remarkable aspect of the book of Nehemiah. Yes – Nehemiah had faith and it was a true faith that he acted on. He made a long and difficult journey from Babylon to Jerusalem. Then, against all odds, he performed an epic work in the Lord rebuilding the wall of Jerusalem. But the remarkable characteristic of Nehemiah is not just his faith or his work. It is his prayer. He prays throughout the book. Almost the whole first chapter is prayer. But the prayer does not stop there:

Neh. 2:4b – "So I prayed to the God of heaven."
Neh. 4:4 - "Hear, O God, how..."
Neh. 4:9 – "But we prayed to our God..."
Neh. 5:19 – "Remember me, O my God..."
Neh. 6:14 – "Remember me, O my God..."
Neh. 7:5 – "Then my God put it in my heart..."

The list goes on. Almost all of Nehemiah 9 is a prayer.

Prayer is the foundation for everything that we do. A disciple connects to the Source through prayer. This life connection is cultivated by time - time spent with the Lord ... time in prayer ... time in meditation ... time in seeking ... time in exaltation.

> PRINCIPLE: A person enters into a relationship with God through prayer.

Nehemiah's prayer demonstrates the relationship that Nehemiah had with the Lord God Almighty. That relationship was the basis for the work of God that Nehemiah accomplished. Nehemiah knew that his relationship with God, and not his political influence, enabled him to restore the community of Jerusalem.

> PRINICIPLE: Our relationship with God empowers us to restore communities around us.

DESIRE AND PRAYER

One time, my young friend Kennedy and I drove to some of the poorer neighborhoods in the city, and began knocking on doors to distribute gift baskets to some needy refugee families. Many of these neighborhoods were isolated enclaves. The neighborhoods were dark and not necessarily "safe" areas. I told Kennedy that some of the places that we went were frightening to me. Kennedy allowed that he was a little scared himself. I was thankful to have him with me.

We came to Peter's house, and gave his family a gift basket. Peter agreed to go with us to some of the other dwellings and to translate as needed. He directed us to a small side road where two of our Boyz Club guys had moved – Linda Street. I had never been there before. As we drove down the drive a few hundred feet, it opened into a huge complex with run down building after run down building where hundreds of people lived. The place looked squalid. Trash was scattered on the ground and over the parking lot. The apartments were filthy. Glass was broken and windows were missing. Storm doors were gone. I shuddered. I sensed darkness.

Peter, who himself lived in an area that I considered dangerous, said, "This place is bad. It is full of drugs."

He then pointed to a group of unkempt young men who gathered on the street corner for no apparent reason and said, "Those guys have guns."

I thought of the Boyz Club guys that lived at Linda Street. Immediately I prayed "Lord, what is Your will for this community? What vision do you have for a place like this one? What hope for people that live in these conditions and are subjected to these

influences? Please send workers to bring light to this neighborhood." I made it a point to return.

By means of consistent and frequent time in prayer, the relationship with God deepens and intimacy develops. The relationship becomes a regular communion. And through that communion, God **transforms** your heart so that your will becomes joined to His will. God's heart touches your heart. God molds the desires of your heart into Godly desires...His desires.

> PRINCIPLE: Through communion with God, God conforms your will to His will.

At this point, you can begin to pray effectively. As God conforms your will to His will, and you begin to understand His will, then you can pray with faith because you have discerned His will. "In that day you will ask in My name, and I do not say to you that I will request the Father on your behalf; for the Father Himself loves you, because you have loved Me, and have believed that I came from the Father." Jn. 16:26-27.

> PRINICIPLE: When your desire and God's desire intersect, then you can petition Him effectively.

Nehemiah had this experience. He discerned God's will through God's word – a promise made many years before to Moses.

"Remember the word which Thou didst command Thy servant Moses, saying, 'If you are unfaithful I will scatter you among the peoples; but if you return to Me and keep My commandments and do them, though those of you who have been scattered were in the most remote part of the heavens, I will gather them from there and will bring them to the place where I have chosen to cause My name to dwell.'" Neh. 1:8-9.

Now that he grasped God's will in the matter, Nehemiah prayed. But Nehemiah didn't just pray. Nehemiah prayed in faith. And Nehemiah prayed fervently. These are the key components to effective prayer – faith and fervor. "The effective prayer of a righteous man can accomplish much. Elijah was a man with nature like ours, and he prayed earnestly (ASV – "fervently") that it might not rain..." Jm. 5:16b-17a. Like Elijah, Nehemiah prayed fervently knowing that God had revealed His will to him. "...let Thine ear now be attentive and Thine eyes open to hear the prayer of Thy servant which I am praying before Thee now day and night..." Neh. 1:6. Because God's will is paramount, the disciple perseveres in fervent prayer until His will is done.

> PRINCIPLE: Effective prayer is fervent prayer in faith in alignment with God's revealed will.

Today, Linda Street is a different place. My friend and coworker, Hunter, has established a ministry apartment there. Daily, the people of God go to that neighborhood and minister – through Bible studies, tutoring, food and clothing ministry, soccer, Taekwondo classes…the list goes on. Linda Street still has problems, but a place that was darkness is now seeing a great light.

I did not do much to impact Linda Street. God called other people to do that work. But years ago I did pray in accordance with God's will for that community.

IDENTIFYING A COMMUNITY

"I prayer walk (Monday-Saturday) the area where our church building is located – God having dealt with me that this area is one of my 'flocks' (Prov. 27:23) and that we are responsible for them. It is a 3-mile walk.

"My original vision was to prayer walk it doing nothing more than worshipping God as I walked. However it quickly, immediately became a ministering, relational development. I now know many of the people, their needs, etc., and some are coming to church (primarily men). It is slowly developing, and who knows what all God is doing through it.

"Since the start of this we have changed from being a church where our Sunday morning services were primarily with white attendees, to where at times the racial makeup is 2-to-1 black – a true reflection of the racial makeup of the neighborhood and the city."

This testimony is given by an uncle of mine – a man who is a pastor in Selma, Alabama. The Lord called him to minister to Selma, Alabama many years ago. Note his understanding of the concept of corporate responsibility – the idea that a body of believers is not just responsible for themselves, but it is responsible for the community around them. The "flock" is not just church members. The flock is the community around the church. Jesus had the heart of a shepherd, and He encouraged His disciples to look beyond their inner circle for the flock. "And seeing the multitudes, He felt compassion for them, because they were distressed and downcast like sheep without a shepherd. Then He said to His disciples. 'The harvest is plentiful, but the workers are few. Therefore beseech the Lord of the harvest to send out workers into His harvest.'" Mt. 9:36-38.

Through prayer, God changed the flock to which my uncle was called. Through prayer, God shows us the call on our lives. Through prayer, God identifies the areas to which a disciple or a group of disciples are called to do His intended work. Then, through prayer, God acts to accomplish His intended work.

This book can not tell you where to go to impact a community. Only the Lord can do that. The Lord will call a person or a body of believers to any place that the Lord desires.

But the first place to look is around you. Many times a church is planted in a location for a reason. Where has the Lord placed you? What is the Lord doing around you? What areas in your city are in need of restoration? The Lord may send you thousands of miles away, but the likely place for the Lord to send you is located right outside your door...or down a small driveway that you have passed everyday that opens into a poor community of hundreds of people.

> PRINCIPLE: The first territory a church should consider is the community around the church.

MEDITATION: "You, O king, were looking and behold, there was a single great statue; that statue, which was large and of extraordinary splendor, was standing in front of you, and its appearance was awesome. The head of that statue was made of fine gold, its breast and its arms of silver, its belly and its thighs of bronze, its legs of iron, its feet partly of iron and partly of clay. You continued looking until a stone was cut out without hands, and it struck the statue on its feet of iron and clay, and crushed them. Then the iron, the clay, the bronze, the silver and the gold were crushed all at the same time, and became like chaff from the summer threshing floors; and the wind carried them away so that not a trace of them was found." Dan. 2:31-35a.

1. How important is the foundation?

2. Do you have a foundation of prayer in your life?

3. How connected do you feel to God as your Source?

4. What steps can we take to pray in accordance with God's revealed will?

5. Are there any areas in your community to which God may be calling you?

REVIEW:
1. Ongoing connection with our Source is essential.
2. We need God's continuous presence in our lives in order to do God's work.
3. A person enters into a relationship with God through prayer.
4. Our relationship with God empowers us to restore communities around us.
5. Through communion with God, God conforms your will to His will.
6. When your desire and God's desire intersect, then you can petition effectively.
7. Effective prayer is fervent prayer in faith in alignment with God's revealed will.
8. The place to consider God's plan for restoration is the area around you.

RELATIONSHIP > INTERCESSION

LESSON THREE – "I AND MY FATHER'S HOUSE HAVE SINNED!"

How do we build a bridge between ourselves and persons from another culture or another class?

I learned the value of young children in cross-cultural ministry. We tend to discount the impact of young children, because – well – they are children. But the more experience I gained in the field, the more I realized the value of the children in the ministry. Admittedly, my realization came through trial and error.

One of the first tasks I performed in our outreach was to visit and welcome refugee families that just arrived in America to our community. I dreaded these visits. The adults spoke little or no English. Their mannerisms were different, and their apartments smelled strange. Communication was difficult. The problem was more me than them though. My talents were simply not geared toward quick connection.

After a few very tense visits, I decided to take my toddler children with me. All the world loves a small child, and when I say "all the world," I mean ALL the world. I knocked on the door of the apartment and a foreign face appeared at the door. The face looked at me with all the apprehension and distrust of a person that had been subjected to inhuman treatment in his native land, was exiled from it, and now lived in a strange and frightening environment. But when the face looked down and saw my young son and daughter, it brightened and relaxed. When the face looked back at me, it had obviously connected me with my children. The expression was a lot friendlier.

A gesture motioned us to come into the apartment. As we walked into the apartment, overtures were made toward my children. Then I sat down and tried to explain who we were and why we were there. More often than not on those visits, young children – children not too much different from my own, lived in the apartment.

My young children were a bridge between two very different cultures and perspectives.

A few weeks later, as I became better acquainted with some families, I asked young

children from those families to accompany me on visits to new families from the same cultures. I had gained a level of trust with the children, mainly through playing soccer with them. Usually, the young children from refugee families spoke much better English than their parents. Then when I knocked on a strange door, I not only had a person from the same culture who acted as a bridge, but I also had a translator. The connection and communication was much easier.

Ultimately, I upgraded one of my primary ministry goals. My initial goal was to educate myself to the point that I could bridge cultural barriers to reach out to other cultures. That goal progressed. A person from the same culture was much more effective than I was. A person from the same culture fully understood the perspectives, background and challenges of his own people. My goal changed. My goal now is to train and grow indigenous ministers who can minister the Gospel to their own people in word and in deed. They are the most effective bridge.

"...let Thine ear now be attentive and Thine eyes open to hear the prayer of Thy servant which I am praying before Thee now, day and night, on behalf of the sons of Israel Thy servants..." Neh. 1:6a.

This is the essence of intercession. To intercede means "to mediate; to stand between." An intercessor acts as a bridge in prayer, just as those children acted as a bridge between two cultures. The intercessor stands between God and other(s), and through prayer, reconciles other(s) to God.

The most effective bridge connects two sides by taking in account the characteristics of both sides. To mediate effectively, a mediator must realize fully the perspective of both parties. "Now a mediator is not for one party only..." Gal. 3:20.

> PRINCIPLE: A mediator must understand the perspectives of both sides.

That is why Jesus is the ultimate mediator. "For there is one God, and one mediator also between God and men, the man Christ Jesus..." I Tim. 2:5. Jesus is God. But he also took fully human form – "the **man** Christ Jesus." Through what He experienced and suffered, He understood the perspectives of God and man intimately. "Hence also, He is able to save forever those who draw near to God through Him, since He always lives to make intercession for them." Heb. 7:25.

In his prayer, Nehemiah touched the heart of God and learned God's intention for his people. But Nehemiah wasn't the only person in Babylon that prayed. Three times a day, Daniel prayed toward Jerusalem. Dan. 6:10. In Daniel 9, Daniel grasped God's plan that the "desolations of Jerusalem" would be completed in seventy years as "revealed" by the prophet Jeremiah. Dan. 9:2. He immediately began interceding for his people in accordance with God's revealed will.

> PRINCIPLE: Effective intercession begins at the point that your heart touches God's heart.

Revelation of God's intentions for a community leads to effective intercession for it. It is a matter of revelation <u>and</u> timing. If Daniel or Nehemiah had begun his intercession for the people of Israel seventy years earlier, that intercession would not have been effective! Seventy years earlier, God told Jeremiah **not** to intercede for his people. "As for you, do not pray for this people, and do not lift up cry or prayer for them, and do not intercede with Me; for I do not hear you." Jer. 7:16. God's revealed will is the key.

But Nehemiah and Daniel also understood the perspective of their people. For Nehemiah, this understanding was underscored by the report that the people of Jerusalem were in "great distress and reproach" and the "wall of Jerusalem is broken down." Neh. 1:3. Now that Nehemiah and Daniel fully grasped the mind of the Lord in the matter, and the plight of their people, they could meaningfully intercede for the community. And they did – night and day.

> PRINCIPLE: The basis for intercession is a revelation of God's will and man's plight.

THE FIRST PRINCIPLE: RESPONSIBILITY

For ten years we held a weekend soccer camp for the refugee youth in the spring. We funded the camp on a shoestring budget. A YMCA camp kindly allowed us to rent its facility for the weekend for a nominal fee. Food, supervision, and transportation were always logistical issues, but we managed it.

The guys loved the camp. Along with the soccer and basketball, they exchanged the confines of urban multi-family housing for open spaces. We allowed the older guys to sleep in a separate cabin from the main building, and they exchanged the strict limitations of home life for sleepless nights of freedom under light supervision.

One morning at the camp though, the YMCA staff person reported that he smelled cigarette smoke in the older guys' cabin. Some one had been smoking, which was an egregious violation of the camp rules. I knew that immediate action was in order.

I called all of the older guys together. I had an idea of the probable culprit. But I needed proof. "Guys," I said "the camp counselor has reported that some one has been smoking. I need to know who it was."

Eyes looked downward. Silence. Finally, Mohamed said "No one was smoking, Coach." I had coached Mohamed. Mohamed was not known for his truthfulness.

"Listen!" I said. "This is the camp counselor who has reported the smoking to me. He does not lie about such things. Some one has been smoking. You know the camp rules. Smoking is a violation of the rules. I need for the person who has been smoking to be brave, to step forward and to be truthful about it."

The guys looked at one another. More silence. No one was going to snitch on a friend.

"Guys," I said "let me tell you why this is important. The YMCA very kindly lets us use this facility every year. They only ask that we take care of it and that we follow their rules. If we don't get to the bottom of this, I am concerned about whether we will be allowed to come back next year. This smoking needs to be addressed. If no one comes forward, then I don't know if we will have another camp. We are not playing soccer or doing anything else until we get an answer."

More silence. I waited for what seemed a very long time. Finally Isak, Mohamed's best friend, spoke up. "Coach," he said "I did it."

I looked at Isak. I had coached Isak as well. I knew that Isak was not the person guilty of smoking.

"Isak?" I asked. "Are you sure?"

Then Ahmed spoke up. "Coach, I did it."

"Coach, I did it." It was Abdul.

"No, coach, I did it." It was Mohamed.

Within a few seconds, it went from no one smoking to everyone smoking – all fifteen guys. Each one of those young men told me that he was the person who smoked.

I stood there and shook my head in amazement. I did not know what to do. To punish the whole crowd would mean punishing innocent persons as well as the guilty person.

Then it hit me. These guys understood what it meant to be community. Even the innocent were willing to take upon themselves the guilt of the community. For the sake of friendship and unity, they assumed the burden of guilt and were willing to suffer its punishment. I respected that. At that point, the "wind was out of my sails." In light of this strong display of community, I lost my resolve to be punitive. I gave a subdued lecture and walked away.

"...let Thine ear now be attentive and Thine eyes open to hear the prayer of Thy servant which I am praying before Thee now, day and night, on behalf of the sons of Israel Thy servants, confessing the sins of the sons of Israel which we have sinned against Thee; I and my father's house have sinned. We have acted very corruptly against Thee..." Neh. 1:6-7a.

"I have sinned." "We have acted very corruptly against Thee." By all accounts, Nehemiah was a righteous man. He walked closely with God, praying regularly. But consider how he prayed. He took the part of his people in confessing their sins against God.

Daniel was likewise a righteous man. But when Daniel prayed, he also confessed the sins of Israel as his own.

"...[W]e have sinned, committed iniquity, acted wickedly, and rebelled, even turning aside from Thy commandments and ordinances...open shame belongs to us, O Lord, to our kings, our princes, and our fathers because we have sinned against Thee..." Dan. 9:5,8a.

"We...us...we." In their intercession, Daniel and Nehemiah demonstrate two significant principles that are necessary for restoration of a community. The first principle is Corporate Responsibility. Corporate responsibility means that a person who is a part of a body, a community, or even a nation, bears its burdens. If there is guilt in a people, as part of that people, the righteous person assumes responsibility for it. It is not that he personally is guilty. As an intercessor, he "steps in between" and addresses it with the Lord "on behalf of" his people, just as Nehemiah and Daniel did.

> PRINCIPLE: We bear responsibility for our community, our city and our people.

When God calls you to perform His work in a community, it is essential that you become a part of that community. You spend time there. Your presence should be felt there. You interact with the people and become involved in their lives. As a part of that community, you bear responsibility for it before the Lord. If there are sins in that community, confess them to the Lord and ask for mercy. If there are needs in that community, bring them before the Lord and seek His provision. If there are unsaved in that community, pray for reconciliation of men to God.

> PRINCIPLE: If God calls you to work in an area, you must assume responsibility for that area.

THE SECOND PRINCIPLE: BROKENNESS

September 11, 2001. Chances are good when you read this date, your mind recalls horrible images – huge clouds of smoke and dust; skyscrapers imploding; and unspeakable perishings.

That September, I was coaching a large number of young men from Arabic countries on my outreach soccer team. Over the next few weeks, those young men described to me the impact of 9/11 on them. At school, fellow students avoided interaction with them and stared at them suspiciously. Isak told me he went to Wal-mart to apply for a job. The manager told Isak that the store was out of employment applications. But as Isak was leaving the store, another person walked by him with an employment application in his hand.

Abdullah was very studious. For years he pursued his dream job, but later told me that he had given up on it. His dream was to be an airline pilot. "Coach" he said "can you imagine what it would be like? 'Good morning, ladies and gentlemen. Welcome to Regent Airlines. This is Abdullah Mohamed speaking. I will be your captain today. We hope that you enjoy your flight.'"

The fall of 2001 was a most difficult season. Other teams played our "foreigners" roughly and violently. The pressures from game to game escalated. Finally four of the players – Mahir, Abdullah, Abdi and Mohamed – lost it. They acted out during a game and then rejected the coach's discipline for it. I had no choice but to kick them off the team. We managed to complete the season with a roster of 12 players, but it was a struggle.

During the offseason, I worked on relationships. These guys had a lot of pride. One by one though, each suspended player contritely approached me and apologized for his actions during the prior season. We discussed what had happened, and how change was needed for proper play and for appropriate attitudes.

The next season was a different season. Assured of a change, I restored 3 of the 4 suspended players to the team. That team won a lot of games, and it played with much better sportsmanship. We were invited to compete in a tournament at season's end. In reality, it was a small tournament. But to my players, it was the "championship."

The team was elated when we won the championship game. But no one was happier than the 3 players that had been suspended the prior year. At the postseason banquet, I took the opportunity to share about redemption.

A number of years later, I saw Abdullah. We hugged and exchanged greetings, and shared updates. Then Abdullah looked at me, and smiled. "Coach" he said "we won the championship in 2002, didn't we?"

"Yes Abdullah," I said. "We won the championship in 2002. But we had to go through the season of 2001 to win the championship in 2002."

Our goal is restoration. The steps to restoration are the same for a community as they are for a person. The first step is acknowledgement of condition. It is recognition of the condition of the community that leads to brokenness. We acknowledge the physical and spiritual deterioration around us to the Lord. Here is the impact on Nehemiah and Daniel:

"...I sat down and wept and mourned for days; and I was fasting and praying before the God of heaven." Neh. 1:4.

"So I gave my attention to the Lord God to seek Him by prayer and supplications, with fasting, sackcloth and ashes." Dan. 9:3.

> PRINCIPLE: Brokenness is a key to restoration.

Here is a necessary realization: The sins of our world today are like the sins of Israel. Our communities have "sinned, committed iniquity, acted wickedly, and rebelled, even turning aside from [the Lord's] commandments and ordinances." Dan. 9:5. As a people, we have rejected the Lord from being God over us. We have listened to our own voices and not to the voice of the Lord our God. Dan. 9:10.

The state of brokenness yields confession. As people responsible to God for the condition of the world around us, we need to confess the sins of our community, our nation and our people to the Lord.

> PRINCIPLE: Out of brokenness comes forth confession.

Look at the community to which you are called. Look at the community around you. What are the sins of that community? Are there drug problems, domestic violence or suicide? Is there luxuriant wealth, greed, self-indulgence or crass commercialism? Is there despair and depression? Are the people self-absorbed and self-gratified? Is there deviance?

Then confess it to the Lord – all of it.

Confession is the foundation of change. Confession invites the Lord to forgive, and then to bring forth change, healing, and restoration.

> PRINCIPLE: Confession leads to change and to restoration.

Nehemiah and Daniel knew that the people of Israel needed restoration. That need led them to brokenness. Nehemiah and Daniel took responsibility for the sins of Israel before the Lord. That responsibility led them to confession. Then, from that foundation, the Lord ordained change leading to restoration.

> Brokenness to confession to change to restoration. It is time to cry out.

MEDITATION: "The people of the land have practiced oppression and committed robbery, and they have wronged the poor and needy and have oppressed the sojourner without justice. And I searched for a man among them who should build up the wall and stand in the gap before Me for the land, that I should not destroy it; but I found none." Eze. 22:29-30.

Read Nehemiah 1. Read Daniel 9. Feel within yourself what Nehemiah and Daniel were feeling.

1. Has God given you a burden for a people or a community around you?

2. What do you think about the idea that a person should take responsibility for and confess the sins of others?

3. In your personal life, have you ever experienced the progression of brokenness, confession, change, and then restoration?

4. What are the sins of your community?

REVIEW:
1. A mediator must understand the perspectives of both sides.
2. The basis for intercession is a revelation of God's will and man's plight.
3. We bear responsibility for our community, our city and our people.
4. If God calls you to work in an area, you must assume responsibility for that area.
5. Brokenness is a key to restoration.
6. Out of brokenness comes forth confession.
7. Confession leads to change and to restoration.

RELATIONSHIP > INTERCESSION > EMPOWERMENT

LESSON FOUR – THE APPOINTED TIME

There was a showdown in Jerusalem.

Nehemiah stood in Jerusalem. He had a daunting task ahead – to rebuild the walls and gates of Jerusalem in order to establish the Lord as its King therein. Not one rock had yet been laid to rebuild. As Nehemiah stood, he was surrounded by the enemies of Jerusalem – powerful enemies who had open access to the city and the temple area; powerful enemies who had subdued the people in Jerusalem and heaped upon them ridicule and reproach.

Now these enemies confronted Nehemiah face to face. "But when Sanballat the Hororite, and Tobiah the Ammonite official, and Gesham the Arab heard it, they mocked us and despised us and said, 'What is this thing you are doing? Are you rebelling against the king?'" Neh. 2:19. It was the first of many showdowns.

How would Nehemiah respond? What would he, the newcomer, say to such a powerfully entrenched group? Nehemiah declared this: "The God of heaven will give us success; therefore we His servants will arise and build, but you have no portion, right, or memorial in Jerusalem." Neh. 2:20.

"The God of heaven will give us success! You have no portion, right, or memorial in Jerusalem!" These are pretty strong words for a neophyte who has not begun his work. Do you feel the strength that underlies these words? Do you sense the authority that supports this response?

What does it take to stand in the midst of enemies surrounded by rubble and to build a wall? What does it take for a leader of slaves like Moses to walk in and to confront the most powerful man on earth demanding "Let my people go"? Ex. 5:1. What does it take to stand in the midst of evil, sin and despair, and to bring the kingdom of God to an area? What does it take to walk into sheer darkness and to flick on a beacon of light to shine in that darkness and to expose it?

It requires an understanding that God Almighty Himself has commissioned the work.

> PRINCIPLE: Nehemiah understood that the Lord had given him authority.

How did Nehemiah know that he had authority in this matter? He knew the authority with which he operated because of what he had already experienced.

THE IMPACT OF CALL

Two little words can make quite a difference! We use words carefully because words have meaning. Two words can completely change the situation.

When my youngest daughter, Maureen, was four years old, she was a cute, sensitive and compliant child. At that time, my oldest child, Jackson, was ten years old. Jackson was large for his age. He towered over Maureen. Jackson had the sense of power, responsibility and will toward his siblings that reflects the status of a first born child.

If Maureen went outside where Jackson was playing and said "Jackson, come on inside," Jackson would pause and look down at Maureen as if she were crazy. Who was Maureen to give Jackson an order? Even if Jackson felt kindly disposed toward Maureen, he would challenge the idea. "Why should I come inside with you?" Maureen would have to use all the tools at her disposal to convince Jackson to come inside, and even then Jackson might decide playing outside was just too much fun.

But on this occasion, Maureen didn't just tell Jackson to "come on inside." I, Jackson's father, had asked Maureen to go tell Jackson to come inside. So four year-old Maureen went alone, but she went with authority from her father. And when she addressed Jackson, she added two little words: "Daddy says..." Maureen said "Jackson, Daddy says come on inside."

Two words can make quite a difference. Jackson didn't look down at Maureen or ignore her. Although little Maureen was the bearer of the command, Jackson understood that the authority of the command was not coming from Maureen, but from a higher

source – a source with authority. Jackson stopped what he was doing, turned, and obediently followed Maureen back into the house.

Jackson obeyed immediately. But some factors existed that compelled him to respond positively.

A CLEAR CALL

First, Jackson heard clearly the call from his father. Maureen delivered the message, but Jackson understood that his father was the source of the message. The direction to Jackson was clear and unequivocal.

When Nehemiah stood and faced his enemies, he also had heard a clear and unequivocal direction. God had called him to rebuild the wall around Jerusalem. "And I arose in the night, I and a few men with me. I did not tell any one *what God was putting into my mind* to do for Jerusalem..." Neh. 2:12.

Nehemiah didn't operate on his own. Through his prayer and intercession, he understood the will of God for him and for the area around him. Nehemiah heard from God.

Nehemiah's call was the basis for authority to do the work.

> PRINCIPLE: The clear call of God is the basis for authority to do God's work.

AUTHORITY

Clearly hearing his father's call was an important part of Jackson's obedience. But the second factor is that Jackson understood the authority of the person issuing the call. Jackson knew the power and authority that his father had in his life.

Jackson had experienced the adverse consequences of disobedience. Jackson had previously received discipline from his father on occasions when he had disobeyed. Jackson knew that his father had the power to compel his obedience.

Knowledge of the source of authority is necessary to act under that authority. Knowledge of God is necessary to act under His authority - Knowledge of Who He is, What He is like, and How He interacts in the affairs of man.

> PRINCIPLE: Knowledge of God is necessary to act under His authority.

Nehemiah knew the Lord Whom he served. Note how the enemies of Israel focused on Nehemiah. "What is this thing **you** are doing? Are **you** rebelling against the king?" Nehemiah's enemies thought that the fight was between them and Nehemiah!

Nehemiah knew differently. Nehemiah knew that the fight was between his enemies and the God that commissioned him to do the work. Note how his response focused on God and His authority, rather than on Nehemiah. "**The God of heaven** will give us success; therefore we **His servants** will arise and build, but you have no portion, right or memorial in Jerusalem." Neh. 2:20.

Nehemiah knew the One that he served. This intimate knowledge enabled Nehemiah to fulfill the call of the One Who sent him.

THE IMPACT OF EMPOWERMENT

The previous story isn't just about young, strapping Jackson. The story is also about four year-old Maureen – cute, sensitive and compliant Maureen. Maureen was the youngest of three children. She was the "baby of the family."

All families have a pecking order. I myself was raised in a family with five children. One day, everyone seemed to be on edge. It was rainy outside, and moods were stormy inside. Our parents were tired, and we children were "cooped up" inside the house. Throughout the day, we got on each other's nerves. On such occasions, the pecking order takes effect. The parents snap at the children. The oldest child snaps at the next oldest child, and it goes right down the line to the youngest child. In those situations, the youngest

child is the recipient of a lot of grief.

After a day filled with arguments and tears, late that afternoon we heard a little voice yelling out on the front porch. We cautiously peered out the window. The youngest child in the family, my four year-old brother, Alan, was standing on the front porch. He was yelling at the cat. The cat sat there a little wide-eyed, listening as Alan described in detail the ways in which the cat had not pleased him. He dressed that cat down right and left.

At least Alan had found an outlet for the many frustrations of the day.

When I became a parent, a pecking order existed among my children too. And Maureen was at the bottom of the heap. When one of her siblings desired Maureen's participation in a game, Maureen seemed powerless to resist. It was as if her siblings controlled her life. Maureen followed them around admiringly and compliantly.

Now consider the impact of authority on little Maureen. When her father said, "Go tell Jackson that I said to come inside," Maureen's demeanor changed. Maureen didn't question the command, nor did she question the source. She knew her father. She immediately turned and went to deliver the message to Jackson. She had been empowered.

Further, Maureen's status changed. She went to Jackson boldly. She didn't approach her much larger brother timidly. She approached him confidently with assurance. Maureen went to her brother with authority. The words "Daddy says..." meant a huge difference to Maureen. She was empowered at that point and she acted boldly and resolutely.

Likewise, God's authority empowers the weak and the poor to withstand the powerful and the oppressive.

THE TIMING OF EMPOWERMENT

The leaders set up a weekend retreat for the guys at Boyz Club. We announced the retreat a few weeks before the scheduled weekend. We told them the time and location for pick up on that Friday. Regular reminders were given.

The day for the retreat came. We drove the vans to the pick up location at the appointed time and met a large group of eager guys. Thien was on the list of participants, but he was not there. We waited a while for him and tried to call him. But we couldn't reach him. Finally, we left without him.

After we drove for an hour, we stopped to eat at a restaurant with the guys. The cell phone of Steven, one of our leaders, rang. He answered it and talked for a couple of minutes. Before he hung up, he said "Sorry, we have already left. We told you the time to meet us. We were there, but you were not."

Steven put his cell phone down. He said "That was Thien. He is standing in the rain in Charlotte at the pick up point with his backpack. He overslept, but still wants to come."

Steven and I looked at each other and shook our heads. We were sorry Thien missed the appointed time, but we couldn't go back and get him. Thien missed the retreat.

When God issues a call, He will empower His servant to fulfill that call. But the timing of the empowerment is crucial. The timing of the empowerment may be different than the communication of the call.

The call to Thien about the retreat went out weeks before the retreat. At that point, he was called to the retreat. But Thien was not empowered to go on the retreat until that Friday at the appointed time. The appointed time was the crucial point that Thien needed to act to obey the call. He needed to be present and ready to go at the appointed time and at the appointed place. But Thien acted at a different time, so he was not empowered. He lost his call.

PRINCIPLE: The timing of empowerment may be different than the communication of the call.

It is essential that a called disciple wait to act until the Lord has empowered him to fulfill his call. Consider Nehemiah's approach carefully.

Because of his prayer and intercession, Nehemiah understood the Lord's will for his people to rebuild Jerusalem. But Nehemiah did not act until the Lord empowered him. Nehemiah prayed and interceded, and continued to serve the king. But it was the king - not Nehemiah - that initiated the matter.

...I took up the wine and gave it to the king. Now I had not been sad in his presence. So the king said to me, "Why is your face sad though you are not sick? This is nothing but sadness of heart." And I said to the king, "Let the king live forever. Why should my face not be sad when the city, the place of my fathers' tombs, lies desolate and its gates have been consumed by fire?" Then the king said to me, "What would you request?" Then I prayed to the God of heaven. Neh. 2:1b-4.

Nehemiah prayed and waited until God moved the king's heart. Then Nehemiah made his request, and the king granted it. "So it pleased the king to send me..." Neh. 2:6b.

All authority belongs to God, and all authority is established by God. Rom. 13:1. Nehemiah allowed God to establish his authority. He did not take matters in his own hands, but he waited until God moved to empower him.

> PRINCIPLE: A godly man waits for God to establish his authority.

Consider again the story of Maureen and her brother. If Maureen had approached her brother five minutes before I told her to tell him to come inside, she would have done so without my authority. For Maureen to say "Daddy says..." at that point would have been presumption. She did not have authority.

If Maureen waited thirty minutes after I told her to deliver my message, she would have been neglectful. When I authorized her to tell Jackson to come inside, I empowered her then, and I expected for her to obey immediately.

Delayed obedience equates with disobedience. At the point that God first empowered the children of Israel to enter and take the land of Canaan, the children of Israel refused because of their fear. Numbers 14. They were disobedient. They did not understand the power and authority of their God. So the Lord rebuked them and withdrew his authorization to enter the land.

On the next day, however, after the Lord forbad it, the children of Israel decided to enter the land. But it was too late. The Lord had removed his empowerment. The delayed obedience was now disobedience. The children of Israel were defeated in a rout.

Like Maureen, Nehemiah knew that he not only had been called, but he had been empowered. As he stood before his enemies, Nehemiah knew that he had been called by God and empowered by God in the right place and at the right time.

But Nehemiah had experienced one more thing that gave him confidence to withstand his enemies.

FAVOR

When Maureen was eight years old, I took my family to visit Yosemite National Park. I had been to Yosemite as a child, and I wanted to show its wonders to my three children. We went in late April and there was some concern about snow. In fact, as we drove through the lofty mountain passes on the way to Yosemite, the roads were lined by banks of snow. The road had been cleared by plows inside of Alpine poles, though, and we were able to make it through to Yosemite Valley.

The first glimpse of Yosemite Valley is stunning. As the car rounds the curve and El Capitan and Half Dome come into view, it is breathtaking. El Capitan is a huge mountain of rock that is larger than the Rock of Gibraltar. Off of El Capitan flows Yosemite Falls, the highest waterfall in North America. That day, we ate a picnic at the base of Yosemite Falls. As my middle child, Annie, noted in her diary, "Yosemite is just wonder after wonder."

My wife had made a reservation for us at a small cottage on the edge of the park. When we talked with the housing manager later that afternoon though, the cottage did not quite match its description. The manager looked at my family, then he said, "We actually have a larger chateau available for the same time period. Let me check and see if we can get you in the chateau for the same price."

And what a chateau it was! Four stories high, the chateau had bedrooms on the first and third levels, with a large living area and kitchen on the second level. But the bottom level was the best surprise. It was a playroom furnished with a ping pong table, foosball

table, games and a TV. It snowed that first night and we were snowbound the next day. But no one minded because the children and I played games for hours.

The third day, there was still snow on the ground, but we ventured out. We drove to the beautiful, rustic Wawonna Lodge for lunch. As we were paying for our meal and were preparing to return to the chateau, the waiter said, "By the way, the Mariposa Redwood Grove opened today for the season. You folks may want to go see it." Our eyes lit up.

The Mariposa Grove is just a few miles from the Wawonna Lodge. It contains massive redwood trees hundreds of feet tall with names like the Grizzly Giant and the Three Graces. One of the most famous trees has a hole cut in the bottom large enough to drive a car through. At the Mariposa Grove, we walked through a wonderland of snow and dripping ice, and marveled at the size and beauty of the largest trees on earth. It was spectacular.

Later that week, when we were driving back across California, I reflected on the visit to Yosemite with my wife. "You know," I said "that was an awesome trip. And I felt as if we were treated like royalty. We experienced favor on that trip to Yosemite."

My wife shook her head knowingly and appreciatively.

Favor is something that you may not deserve. But God gives favor to those who follow Him and obey Him.

Nehemiah experienced favor. Not only did the king grant Nehemiah's request to allow him to rebuild Jerusalem, but he also gave Nehemiah tools that he needed to fulfill God's call. The king gave Nehemiah letters to the provincial governors granting him safe passage in the long trek from Babylon to Jerusalem. Neh. 2:7. He instructed the keeper of the king's forest to supply wood that Nehemiah needed to rebuild the walls, the temple and his house. Neh. 2:8. The king supplied an armed escort to accompany Nehemiah and his men on the dangerous journey from Babylon to Jerusalem. Neh. 2:9.

If Nehemiah had acted on his own when he sensed God's call, he would have lacked these tools to fulfill his mission. But Nehemiah waited for God to act, and so he experienced the favor of God's empowerment. Nehemiah knew that "...the king granted them to me because the good hand of my God was with me." Neh. 2:8.

So when he reached Jerusalem, Nehemiah could testify of the Lord's favor on his enterprise to the residents. "And I told them how the hand of my God had been favorable to me, and also about the king's words which he had spoken to me. Then they said, 'Let us arise and build.'" Neh. 2:18.

And Nehemiah could face his enemies. The enemies saw another weak politician who had come with lofty intentions, but with little apparent power. The enemies challenged Nehemiah.

What the enemies did not realize is that this man, Nehemiah, had been called and empowered, and had already experienced the good favor of his God, the Lord Almighty. Because of what Nehemiah had experienced, he was able to face his enemies and proclaim, "The God of heaven will give us success; therefore we His servants will arise and build, but you have no portion, right, or memorial in Jerusalem." Neh. 2:20. For Nehemiah, God's empowerment was the difference between success and failure.

MEDITATION: "Now behold, I have made you today as a fortified city, and as a pillar of iron and as walls of bronze against the whole land, to the kings of Judah, to its princes, to its priests and to the people of the land. And they will fight against you, but they will not overcome you, for I am with you to deliver you," declares the Lord. Jer. 1:18-19.

1. Have you acted with authority from the Lord on any occasion?

2. How did you know that you had authority from Him at that time?

3. Have you ever experienced a call from God to do something, but you had to wait until He empowered you to do it?

4. Describe a time in your life when you have experienced favor.

5. How important in ministry is the foundation of call, empowerment and authority?

REVIEW:

1. Nehemiah understood that the Lord had given him authority.

2. The clear call of God is the basis for authority to do God's work.

3. Knowledge of God is necessary to act under His authority

4. When God issues a call, He empowers His servant to fulfill that call

5. The timing of empowerment may be different than the timing of the call.

6. A godly man waits for God to establish his authority.

7. God gives favor to those who follow Him and obey Him.

8. Nehemiah waited for God to act, and so he experienced the favor of God's empowerment.

RELATIONSHIP > INTERCESSION > EMPOWERMENT > SURVEY

LESSON FIVE – THE SURVEY

Does God call a person or a group of people to minister to the people in a certain area? Through the leading of the Holy Spirit, is a group sent (a "mission") to a country, to a city, or even to just one neighborhood?

OBJECT. The China Inland Mission was formed under a deep sense of China's pressing need, and with an earnest desire, constrained by the love of CHRIST and the hope of His coming, to obey His command to preach the Gospel to every creature. Its aim is, by the help of GOD, to bring the Chinese to a saving knowledge of the love of GOD in CHRIST, by means of itinerant and localised work throughout the whole of the interior of China.

This statement is the beginning of a summary of core values of the China Inland Mission written by Hudson Taylor. Hudson Taylor was called to China in 1854. He spent 51 years in ministry there. Under Hudson Taylor's leadership, China Inland Mission brought over 800 missionaries to China. They began 125 schools and their efforts resulted in over 18,000 conversions as well as the establishment of more than 300 stations of work. (Source: Wikipedia and www.omf.org)

"So I went out at night by the Valley Gate in the direction of the Dragon's Well and on to the Refuse Gate, inspecting the walls of Jerusalem which were broken down and its gates which were consumed by fire." Neh. 2:13.

Nehemiah was called to Jerusalem – to rebuild it and to reestablish the Lord as its King. After the Lord called him and empowered him, Nehemiah journeyed there. But he did not start work immediately. First, he surveyed the site of the work. He went out at night with just a few men and inspected the state of the walls and gates of Jerusalem. His survey showed him a number of things.

DEFINITION OF TERRITORY

First, Nehemiah's survey helped him to DEFINE THE TERRITORY. Like many major ancient cities, Jerusalem had gradually grown over the years. As the city grew, its walls expanded. Jerusalem had inner walls and gates and outer walls and gates. Nehemiah had to decide which walls and gates to rebuild. The survey helps to answer the question: Where do we need to build the "wall?" Where do we need to minister?

> PRINCIPLE: The survey helps to define the territory for ministry.

THE CONDITION

The second key that a survey reveals is THE CONDITION OF THE TERRITORY. Nehemiah saw that some parts of the wall were partially broken. Other parts were so utterly destroyed that his mount could not pass through the rubble. Neh. 2:14.

The survey of the area identifies the issues and problems in the area. What problems do we need to address? What obstacles in the lives of the people and the community do we need to overcome?

> PRINCIPLE: The survey of the area identifies the issues and problems in the territory.

RAFA'S VIEW

Here is the experience of a ten year old child:

My family is pretty poor. My daddy went to jail when I was four. I haven't seen him since. I got six brothers and sisters. My mom cares for us, but I am hungry a lot.

We all live in an apartment with 2 bedrooms and 1 bathroom. The bathroom breaks

a lot and it smells bad. I sleep on the floor in a room with my 3 brothers. We have a lot of bugs in our place. My mom works hard cleaning other people's homes, so we don't see her much except at night.

A lot of people live in our building. I play outside all day near where we live, and my clothes get dirty. But the thing I hate most is when I am hungry. Most times I don't eat breakfast. My older brothers and sisters eat most of our food. Some times we run out of food and don't have anything to eat for supper.

One day a man came into our neighborhood and passed out some papers. He gave me a paper and said it was going to be fun. I couldn't read the paper, so I took it home to my older sister. She said the paper said something about a carnival the next Saturday at a park near our apartment. The carnival had games, food and prizes. It sounded like something that me and my friends would like to go to.

The next Saturday some of us walked to the park for the carnival. There were places set up with games and loud music. A lot of people were dressed in funny costumes and there were balloons everywhere. The people gave us free food like hot dogs, chips, sodas and candy. I ate lots of candy. My friends and me played games and had a lot of fun. We could go from place to place and play a game. Every time we did, we got some food or a little toy. I put a bunch of candy in my bag to take home with me.

Then near the end the carnival people called every one together. A man got up to speak. He talked into a wire that made his voice real loud. He started talking about a guy named Jesus. He told us that Jesus loved us. I had heard about love from my older sisters. The man said that Jesus cared for us and wanted us to belong to him.

Then the man told a story about a mother chicken. The chicken had baby chickens that got attacked by a snake. But the mother chicken tried to save the baby chickens. The snake bit the mother chicken and the mother chicken died. The man said all of us were like baby chickens. Jesus was like the mother chicken that died so she could save her baby chickens.

The man asked how many of us wanted to get love from Jesus. He said it was really important to know Jesus. He said it was the most important thing we could do. He asked us to raise our hands if we wanted Jesus. The other carnival people acted like they really

wanted us to raise our hands. I liked the carnival and I liked the food and toys they gave me. I thought that these must be great people to know. Me and our friends raised our hands which made the carnival people happy. They clapped their hands. Then the man closed his eyes and said some words. The man stopped talking and the carnival people shook my hand. An old woman hugged me. She said she loved me.

Me and my friends went home. I ate as much of my candy as I could, but my brothers and sisters took most of it. It was gone by the next day. The next few days I did the same stuff I always do. I played outside and I was hungry a lot. My life didn't change. I never saw the carnival people again. I wish they would come back and bring me more food and candy.

I am not sure about love or what it is. My older sisters talk about love when they go out and meet some guys in the evening. But I am not sure love means a lot because those guys don't stay around. The carnival people talked about love, but they never came back either.

During the survey of the issues within the territory, remember that the gospel applies to the whole person. We preach a gospel of salvation. The gospel is "the power of God for salvation to every one who believes..." Rom. 1:16.

But the gospel impacts every part of a person – spirit, soul, mind and body. Godly ministry in love is not just spiritual. It is physical as well. "If a brother or sister is without clothing and in need of daily food, and one of you says to them, 'Go in peace, be warmed and be filled,' and yet you do not give them what is necessary for their body, what use is that?' Even so faith, if it has no works, is dead, being by itself." Jm. 2:15-17.

It is remarkable how Jesus was careful to minister to the whole person. Jesus not only forgave the sins of the paralytic, but He also healed him. Mk. 2. He refused to send the hungry 5,000 away as his disciples urged. Mt. 14:15. Instead, Jesus met their physical need and fed the 5,000, even though they would later withdraw and not walk with Him any more. Jn. 6:26, 66. Jesus even addressed the physical need of the rich, young ruler – he had tangible excess. Mk. 10:21. (Sometimes need is caused by too much rather than too little.)

All things have a spiritual basis. Many times physical poverty accompanies spiritual poverty. The gospel addresses both types of poverty.

The survey accounts for the condition of the territory in holistic terms – spiritual and physical; emotional and tangible. A proper assessment of needs includes the personal, bodily and human needs of the people of the community.

My church defined an area around it that it wanted to impact. We obtained detailed information about the area – information about its people (demographics), its economic status, its neighborhoods, its schools and its recreation. Here are some factors that we found:

1. **The population density was one of the highest in the city.**
2. **The area was transitional – almost 60% of the population rented their housing.**
3. **The area had a high poverty rate - unemployment at the time was almost twice the national average.**
4. **There were more households of single parents with children than married parents with children.**
5. **Crime rates far exceeded the average rate of crime in the city.**
6. **Hopelessness was rampant. The suicide rate was over double the national average.**

In response, my church initiated action to meet some of the physical needs of the community that we identified. For example, we started a Food Pantry to help poor families that did not have enough to eat. We also committed to pray about crime in the area. We prayed about the crime privately, and we prayed against the crime as we prayer walked through the identified area.

THE RESOURCES

The third key highlighted by a survey of the territory is AN ASSESSMENT OF RESOURCES. The survey of resources tells you the existing tools that you have for the work. The available resources are a factor in development of a plan and in determination of the methods that you will use to impact the community. The survey helps to answer the question: How do we do it?

> PRINCIPLE: The survey of resources helps to answer the question: How do we do it?

A survey of resources looks at resources that you have. What does your church or ministry own that might be useful? Nehemiah had a grant of wood from the king as a resource that he could use. But Nehemiah did not only look at his own resources.

Nehemiah also reviewed the site itself for resources. There was a lot of rubble where a wall used to sit. But even rubble can be useful in rebuilding a wall.

For many years, we have conducted a weekly outreach in a very poor apartment complex full of international refugees. We play soccer with the young men, and then invite them into our apartment for Bible study and fellowship. We call the group "Boyz Club."

When we came into the apartment complex, there was not any space to use as a soccer field. Behind some of the apartment buildings was a swimming pool that had been closed for years. Beside the pool was a former tennis court surrounded with a high fence and covered with sand. Two large metal posts had been installed to hold a net, so the area could be used for volleyball. We did not know where to play soccer.

We bought two portable soccer goals and set them up on the tennis/volleyball court. On the court, we began to play "cage soccer" each week. The "pit," as we call it, has some issues. As many as forty young men at a time play soccer in that tiny area. It is so crowded a person can barely move. Sand flies as the young men kick at the ball. When the wind blows in the dry summer, a cloud of sand billows up from the area. One week, an adult leader had to see a doctor after sand was kicked into his eye.

But the "pit" works. The young men view it as their "home field." When we arrive at the apartments every Wednesday, the young men are there on the "pit" waiting to play soccer.

In assessing resources, look at the community itself. What does the community have that might be useful? Look at buildings, open areas, parks, and schools. Inquire about existing programs and events in the community. Who are the leaders in the community? What are they doing? How do they function?

"Then I passed on to the Fountain Gate and the King's Pool, but there was no place for my mount to pass." Neh. 2:14.

In his survey, Nehemiah found extreme decay. And his resources were scarce. But the provision of the Lord is simply astounding. Needs are often met using "paltry" resources. David was inspired to use five stones as a resource to kill a giant, and to defeat a nation.

Our outreach ministry operates on a "shoestring" budget. We don't have a major supporter or a primary backer. Much of the money for the ministry comes from the pockets of the workers. I am amazed at what is accomplished from our paltry resources.

One of our workers donated a used van to transport the young people. Every week at Boyz Club, I bring the drinks for the guys. Another leader, Patrick, brings a snack. When we go on a retreat, the ministry leaders fund the gas, the food, and prizes.

Every summer we try to send a large number of city youth to Christian camp. One year, a church donated enough money to send 15 teenagers to camp and another ministry raised enough money to send 10 teenagers to camp. Individuals gave money. But we had 70 young people that wanted to go to Doe River Gorge Christian Camp in eastern Tennessee. We told the camp staff that we only had money to pay for 25 young people. The camp said to bring everyone anyway.

The camp sent out a fundraising request to its supporters for our inner city kids. Within a week, the camp's supporters had donated over $30,000.00 for the young people to attend camp. What a blessing!

If God has called you to minister in an area, don't despair of its issues or problems. Look at the resources that are available or potentially available, and ask God for a plan. Many times the plan grows and changes as you begin to work in the area. And many times resources come from an unexpected source. God will provide.

> PRINCIPLE: If God provides the plan, He will provide the resources to complete it.

Finally, be sure to inquire and find out if existing ministries are already working in the community. There is no need to reinvent the wheel. If these ministries or churches exist, connect with them. Meet with them, and understand their vision, motivation and methods. Listen to their leaders and learn from their experience in the community. Explore partnership and coordination with them. The Lord may already be working through His saints in the community. Maybe your role is to assist them.

Nehemiah faced a gargantuan task. The Lord called him to rebuild the walls and gates of Jerusalem from burned rubble. He had limited resources: There was broken down rubble, and there was a grant of wood from the king. But the Lord showed Nehemiah two other major resources that enabled him to form a plan.

PRAYER WALKING

First, Nehemiah knew that the Lord was his resource. We have already shown that Nehemiah was a man of prayer. Throughout the work in Jerusalem, Nehemiah availed himself of the resource of prayer.

My friend, Barney, is married to a woman of prayer, and he is a man of prayer. For a number of months, Barney and his wife walked through their neighborhood. And as they walked through their neighborhood, they prayed for it.

Barney and I attend the same church. Barney, however, had been reading about home fellowship groups and home churches.

A winter storm hit the region. Snow and ice blanketed the city. Sunday services at churches everywhere, including our church, were cancelled. People were "snowed in."

Barney felt God call him to act. Here is what Barney told me:

"After we got the call on Saturday that church was cancelled, I talked with my wife. We felt led to go knock on doors in our neighborhood and to invite our neighbors to come

to our house on Sunday morning for fellowship and worship. So I went out in the cold and ice Saturday night and invited our neighbors to come to our house the next morning.

"I didn't know who would come. But a number of our neighbors walked to our house and we had 12 or so people. We served refreshments, talked, and then had a time of sharing. Some of our neighbors shared some awesome things. Everyone seemed to enjoy the fellowship.

"But that is not the best part. One of our neighbors has an adult son living at home. He has been through a divorce and moved back home to look for work. As everybody was leaving, he seemed to hang back. He said that he wanted to talk to me and my wife.

"After everyone left, we sat down with this young man. He poured his heart out to us. He used to be a Christian, but he had strayed from the Lord. He knew he needed restoration of his relationship with the Lord. We shared with him, and then we prayed with him to be renewed and restored to the Lord. It was such a blessing!"

I paused for a minute and looked at Barney. "You were faithful to do something very inconvenient and to go out in the cold and invite people. You had church at your house.

"But more importantly, I think that the Lord honored your prayer walking. Those prayers for the neighborhood were answered through your neighbors' response. And now a sheep that had gone astray has returned to the fold. What a blessing!"

Barney shook his head knowingly. "My wife and I just rejoiced!" he said.

During the time of the survey, and as the work is being done, prayer walking in the territory of the work is vital to success. Prayer walking does a number of things:

1. <u>Prayer walking takes the presence of God wherever a disciple goes.</u> The presence of God establishes authority in an area. By prayer walking, the church takes charge of the spiritual landscape, and changes it through prayer.

> PRINCIPLE: Prayer walking blesses the community because it brings the presence of God into the community.

2. <u>Prayer walking enhances discernment about the territory.</u>

We have a man in our neighborhood that walks through the neighborhood regularly. Strolling through the neighborhood appears to be Dave's preferred activity. Dave makes his rounds at least 2 or 3 times a day. We call him our "neighborhood walker."

Dave knows more about our neighborhood than anybody else. If I want to know what is going on in the area, I just stop Dave as he walks by our house and I ask him. When a family moves, if a crime was committed, or if a neighbor went to the hospital, Dave knows all about it. Dave is familiar with every person that lives in the neighborhood. (He also knows the most current weather forecast.) Dave is a wealth of information because he covers the area in which he lives with his presence.

When a disciple walks and prays through an area, he discerns things about the area and its people. This discernment is both physical and spiritual. When a Christian is in an attitude of prayer, the Lord reveals His will and His word to him. When a Christian prayerfully walks through an area, he sees people and things that need prayer. Prayer walking expands the scope of prayer and ministry.

> PRINCIPLE: Prayer walking expands the scope of prayer and ministry.

3. <u>Prayer walking enhances interaction with the community and its people.</u> In my neighborhood, Dave knows every one because he sees them and interacts with them. When a Christian prayer walks, he comes into contact with the people of the community. As the Christian obediently goes out, God will bring people into his path that he needs to pray for; people that he will speak with; and people he will minister to.

That is what happened to Peter and John. They were walking to the temple one day for the purpose of prayer. Acts 3:1. But Peter and John never got there. The Lord put a lame man in their path that the Lord healed through their ministry. On the day of Pentecost, 3,000 souls came to the Lord. On the occasion of Peter and John's walk to prayer, 5,000 people believed on the

Lord. Acts 4:4.

Prayer walking is a great first step for a Christian that struggles to reach out – the shy Christian. If you can pray and if you can walk, you can prayer walk. Just walk and pray. The disciple is not required to speak to any one or engage in conversation. But as the Christian routinely prayer walks with faith that the Lord works through his prayer, interaction will come.

> PRINCIPLE: If you can pray and if you can walk, you can prayer walk.

But remember the example of Peter and John. To the extent possible, prayer walk in teams. Team ministry is the Biblical model. Jesus sent His disciples out in teams. Lk. 10:1. Prayer walking in teams is important for unity, support, confirmation and safety.

Some of the elderly persons in our body can't walk long distances. So many of them "prayer drive." They drive through the territory and pray, making stops to pray and bless along the way at key intersections and key locations such as schools, police and fire stations, malls and television stations.

ONGOING WORK

Prayer walking is important, just as the survey of the community is important. Through the information and insight gathered from the survey, the Lord gave Nehemiah a plan to rebuild the walls and gates of Jerusalem. But as the Lord reveals His plan, the prayer walking and the survey should never stop. The needs of the community change, so the prayer focus and the plan change and develop. But always use the resource of prayer.

And don't be discouraged if the survey of resources yields little help. Nehemiah did not have many resources. Jerusalem had been ransacked and its wealth had long ago been plundered by Babylon. But Nehemiah knew that God had authorized and favored the work. He knew the Lord would provide the resources – from somewhere. And the Lord showed him a second major resource.

MEDITATION: "There is a lad here, who has five barley loaves, and two fish; but what are these for so many people?" Jn. 6:9

1. Do you agree that ministry of the gospel is both spiritual and physical? Why or why not?

2. Have you ever had a situation in which God used an unusual resource for ministry?

3. In what ways are you required to trust God for unseen provision in your life?

4. How important to the community is the presence of God's saints in the community?

5. Can you think of reasons why consistency in prayer walking is difficult?

REVIEW:
1. The survey helps to define the territory for ministry.
2. The survey of the area identifies the issues and problems in the territory.
3. The survey accounts for the condition of the territory in holistic terms.
4. The survey of resources helps to answer the question: How do we do it?
5. Prayer walking takes the presence of God wherever a disciple goes.
6. Prayer walking enhances discernment about the territory.
7. Prayer walking enhances interaction with the community and its people.
8. If you can pray and if you can walk, you can prayer walk.
9. To the extent possible, prayer walk in teams.
10. The prayer walking and the survey should never stop.

QUESTIONS TO CONSIDER

Here are some questions to consider in formulating a plan to reach a community:

1. How do we connect with people of the community and establish relationships with them?

2. What programs or events will promote sharing with the people of the community?

3. How do we meet the needs of the community and address the problems that exist in it?

4. How can we establish a permanent presence in the community?

5. How can we encourage long term, lasting discipleship for the people of the community?

6. Who are the leaders in the community with whom we need to make a connection?

RELATIONSHIP > INTERCESSION > EMPOWERMENT > SURVEY > PLAN

LESSON SIX – THE PLAN

Then I said to them, "You see the bad situation we are in, that Jerusalem is desolate and its gates burned by fire. Come, let us rebuild the wall of Jerusalem that we may no longer be a reproach." Neh. 2:17.

The Transcontinental Railroad was one of the greatest engineering feats in American history. It was the line that connected a nation. Authorized by an Act of Congress in 1862, the building of the railroad was a joint operation of government and private enterprise. The government provided land grants and $60,000,000.00 in loans to fund the work. The railroad companies provided expertise, experience and engineering. When it was finished, a cross country journey that previously took the American citizen months could be completed within a few days.

Starting in California, the Central Pacific Railroad began laying tracks eastward. In the Midwest, the Union Pacific Railroad built its railroad westward. Each day, rails were added to the previous day's work and extended the line a little further. Some days yielded scant results. On other days, miles of track were laid. Through deserts, over mountains and across rivers, the construction slowly progressed as track was added to track. The work required hundreds of surveyors and engineers, and tens of thousands of construction laborers.

The railroads faced huge obstacles. Land had to be acquired. Danger abounded in the form of wild animals, inclement weather, faulty equipment and hostile Native Americans who saw the railroad as an intrusion on their lands. Many men died in accidents and attacks. But the railroads pushed toward each other.

Construction of the two railroad tracks started 1,775 miles apart. But they unrelentingly crept toward each other until finally, on May 10, 1869, the two lines met at Promontory, Utah. Two locomotives moved up until they touched each other, and in the presence of 1,100 witnesses, the completion of the "greatest railroad on earth" was

announced.

Start from Point A and build to Point B and then build to Point C. That is how to build a railroad, a highway - or even a wall. Let the treasury fund it. Acquire the land, purchase the materials, and pay the professionals to build it one section at a time. That is how to build - with professionals.

But Nehemiah didn't have a treasury to fund the work. He didn't have a team of professionals or the money to pay them even if he did. Worse still, he didn't have control of the area of the work. Jerusalem's enemies roamed the city at will - intimidating and oppressing its people. How could Nehemiah build a wall with such limited resources?

OUT OF RUBBLE

Nehemiah prayerfully surveyed Jerusalem. He had few physical resources. He had rubble and he had wood from the king. But in the midst of rubble, God can reveal a plan to build.

> PRINCIPLE: In the midst of rubble, God can give a plan.

God showed Nehemiah one more major resource: people. The labor to build the wall came from the people of Jerusalem itself. It was unskilled and untrained labor, but it was labor that was effective nonetheless.

> PRINCIPLE: God showed Nehemiah the resource of people.

God gave Nehemiah a plan under which every citizen of Jerusalem would participate in building the wall. Instead of professionals building from Point A to Point B to Point C, groups of citizens would be assigned to work on every section of the wall at the same time. Nehemiah formed the people into units – teams, as it were. Each team was assigned the task of rebuilding a specific section of the wall. The groups worked together on the whole wall simultaneously.

APPLICATION OF NEHEMIAH'S MODEL

There are many different models for ministry. Each model has strengths and weaknesses, and has to change continuously to meet the need and requirements for effective ministry at the moment. But Nehemiah's model is well-suited for building into the communities around us.

Here is the application of Nehemiah's wall building plan:

A. <u>Each section of the wall represents a different neighborhood, community or area.</u>

God called Nehemiah to rebuild the wall that protected all of Jerusalem. This task was too large for a few builders. But a few builders could rebuild one small section of the wall. So Nehemiah "broke it down." He assigned each team to a section to rebuild. (See Nehemiah 3)

God has called us to bring His kingdom to our cities and communities. That task is too large for a few committed believers. But those believers can take responsibility and build in the neighborhoods and communities in which they live or worship.

This model underscores a core principle in our ministry. We believe that to achieve ministry to the heart, small groups are more effective than large groups. Large groups are effective for encouragement, worship, and even certain forms of teaching. But to dig deeply, to minister personally, and to disciple meaningfully, small groups (or one on one) are required.

Here is our method: **Each person disciples a few people.** Jesus showed the world this model. At times, Jesus ministered to large crowds. But He chose, nurtured, discipled, and trained 12 men. His fundamental method was to make disciples who make disciples. No person can singlehandedly disciple large crowds at the same time. [See <u>THE CALL (Book One – Functional)</u> for a detailed treatment of this form of ministry.] Deep impact occurs with only a few.

For this reason, we encourage our leaders to look for a few people to disciple in the areas in which they minister. We have large community events. But as we draw and assimilate large numbers, our encouragement to our leaders is to see what relationships they develop. Who among the crowd has a desire for the Lord? Who wants to go deeper in Him? Grab hold of those people and spend time with them. Bring them up in the Lord. Help them grow and train them in ministry. Ground your work in relationship, not numbers or flashiness. Each person should do what they have the capability to do.

> PRINCIPLE: Each leader disciples a few people.

How do we make disciples of Jesus? One person at a time. How do we change a city? One neighborhood or community at a time.

B. <u>The people performed the work in teams.</u>
Nehemiah formed small groups to build the wall. Each group worked in a specific section of the wall with a common goal in mind – to rebuild their assigned section of the wall.

> PRINCIPLE: Nehemiah organized task-based groups to build the wall.

I have participated in small groups for over 30 years. Small groups are good for personal encouragement, nurture and care. They offer a depth of intimacy that is not available in large crowds.

My wife and I met in one group for five years. We developed some close friends in that group. I noticed through those years though, that we became "cliquish." It was as if we had our own little club that met to the exclusion of outsiders. The group slowly dwindled until it stopped meeting. Since the group did not reach out, it turned inward, shriveled and died.

Because of that experience, I encouraged our next small group to reach out. As an outlet, we visited a nursing home once a month. It was good ministry and we developed relationships with some of the elderly people in the nursing home. Our group did not have a "call" to that ministry though. Ultimately, the visitation stopped.

My wife and I now meet in a "task-based" small group. Each person in our group feels called to minister to the community near our church, and participates in that ministry. We call it the Neighborhood Outreach small group. When we meet, we report on

the ministry, encourage each other, and coordinate our efforts.

Most importantly, we pray. Prayer is a primary focus of that group. We pray for each other and we pray for the people and ministry. Once a month, we go prayer walking together in the neighborhood of our ministry.

Our Neighborhood Outreach small group has met for 9 years. The fact that we have a common mission – a common call from the Lord – is like a glue that binds us. Our spiritual lives are not diminishing, because we each are outward reaching. We are thriving.

God has formed us into an effective team.

Note the value of a task-based group. Many churches encourage and form small groups to meet during the week. The small group format is meaningful because a small group is much more personal, intimate and effective than a large group. But if the only goal of the group is to meet and support each other, the group eventually becomes stale. My first small group at my church was inward focused. It turned into a social club, and died.

Jesus calls his disciples not only to grow, but to produce fruit. A small group should be fruitful as well. The group that I meet in now has a common goal – outreach into our community. We are active in ministry and we are fruitful. We are alive!

> PRINCIPLE: Task-based small groups can be very fruitful.

Note the effectiveness of task-based groups. United teams are so much more effective than individuals. An individual has a few resources. Teams have manifold resources. One person can only handle a few tasks or relationships. A team can handle many. One person is isolated and alone. A team can encourage and support its members.

Nehemiah understood the value of teams. He divided the people into teams and assigned a common task. In the Nehemiah model, every team building a different section of the wall represents a different ministry or church – or better yet, a consortium of churches and ministries. Multiple teams were required to accomplish the work.

It is preferable that every church build in the community in which it is located. A church that understands its responsibility for the people near it and that acts on that responsibility – that church is a blessing! Often though, a church is inward-focused - more concerned about its own organization and operation than about the life around it. In that instance, a ministry or concerned group of people may need to step in the gap and to build in that community.

> PRINCIPLE: Each team represents a ministry or a church, or better yet, a consortium.

C. Each team worked on its section of the wall, but worked collaboratively with other teams on the wall.

Collaboration is essential to effective ministry. In Nehemiah, each group in the wall was dependent on the group next to it. If one group ran out of stones, mortar, wood or even labor, they had to rely on the group working next to them for help. The groups had to work cooperatively - if for no other reason, because their section of the wall had to join the sections next to it.

Because we live in highly transitional areas, and because our ministry partners meet different needs such as education, recreation, and food distribution, our ministries overlap at times. The growth of Vit, one of our participants, is an example of this dynamic.

When he was younger, Vit lived in the Boyz Club area and attended Boyz Club faithfully. Vit moved though, and began to play on a soccer team sponsored by One7 Ministries, one of our partner ministries. He did not attend Boyz Club very much.

Vit experienced substantial problems in his school studies. Our ministry friend, Hunter, placed him in a tutoring program which Hunter was then running, and began to work with him. Hunter and his team devoted hundreds of hours teaching Vit and helping him work through problems at school and at home.

If the Boyz Club leaders operated territorially, we would protect our turf. A loss of members weakens our ministry. We would confront One7 and Hunter about "stealing" members such as Vit.

But Vit needed what One7 and Hunter offered. We trusted our ministry partners

that they ministered to Vit effectively. Furthermore, we knew that if we had a relationship with Vit, that relationship would survive.

Over the past year, I have noticed that Vit has returned to Boyz Club. In fact, he has become one of our Boyz Club youth leaders.

Each of our ministry partners works within a task-based group – a team. Working with a small group of ministers is manageable and effective.

Perhaps the most Christlike aspect of these ministries though, is that they work together with the other ministries. The ministry leaders meet regularly to encourage each other, to coordinate efforts and to support each other. We hold a monthly outreach leaders' luncheon. We pray for one another. If one ministry experiences a need, we react to meet it.

The unity of our efforts increases our impact on our community.

In our ministry, we try to work cooperatively with each other. We work cooperatively with outsiders. We work cooperatively with other churches.

D. <u>Many teams were citizen-led</u>.

Nehemiah and the people of Jerusalem did not have the luxury of professionals. There was too much work and there were too few professionals.

The work of building into a community is a massive work. It requires hundreds of relationships. The work is too extensive and too intensive to expect trained professionals to do it all. Church leaders are a great resource and they can provide invaluable guidance, leadership and assistance. But our pastors are overloaded with their work as it is. All believers must be called to ministry work.

Many ministries must be led by ordinary people - ordinary citizens like you and like me. Remember the American Revolution. Most American soldiers were ordinary citizens who fought professional soldiers from the most powerful empire on earth. The American citizens believed in a cause, and they were willing to sacrifice for their belief. They overcame incredible odds and obstacles to establish freedom for their communities and families. They also became pretty good soldiers in the process.

Nehemiah's plan was either inspired, or it was desperate. But the plan had requirements.

The building could succeed IF everyone would participate in the building, and IF each person would be faithful to build his part of the wall.

My dental hygienist went on a missions trip to Guatemala. One church that she visited in Guatemala had about 200 members. The vision of the church is to reach young people. The church ministers to children. The church feeds and teaches 1700 children. They plan to disciple the children to adulthood and then to release 1700 ministers of the gospel.

How does a church of 200 people feed and disciple 1700 children? Every member of the church works hard in the ministry.

The pastor of the church says "There are other churches in Guatemala City that are huge. There is nothing wrong with big churches, but often people come to big churches and just sit and listen. In our church, a member comes in and we expect him to work. If a new member comes, we give that member 6 months to see and experience the ministry of the church. After 6 months, that member needs to decide where they are called to work and then get to work.

"If that member is not working after 6 months, then we tell that member something. We tell him 'WE NEED YOUR SEAT!'"

MEDITATION: "Truly, truly, I say to you, he who believes in Me, the works that I do shall he do also; and greater works than these shall he do; because I go to the Father." Jn. 14:12

1. To whom does this declaration apply?

2. How does this verse apply to you?

3. Describe a situation in which you worked as a member of a team. How was that dynamic different than working alone?

4. Do you struggle with the idea that ministries can be "citizen-led?" Why or why not?

5. Why was it important that every person in Jerusalem participate in the work of building in the wall?

REVIEW:

1. In the midst of rubble, God can give a plan.
2. If God provides the plan, He will provide the resources to complete it.
3. God showed Nehemiah the resource of people.
4. Nehemiah organized task-based groups to build the wall.
5. Each section of the wall represents a different neighborhood, community or area.
6. Each leader disciples a few people.
7. Every team building a different section of the wall represents a different church or ministry.
8. Each team worked independently on its section, but worked collaboratively with other teams on the wall.
9. There are different ministries, but they work cooperatively.
10. Many teams are citizen-led.
11. Nehemiah's plan required every citizen to participate in the work of building.

RELATIONSHIP > INTERCESSION > EMPOWERMENT> SURVEY > PLAN

LESSON SEVEN – TWO CULTURES

"For I know the plans that I have for you," declares the Lord, "plans for welfare and not calamity to give you a future and a hope." Jer. 29:11.

I attended a Christian high school graduation recently. The school asked each graduate to select a "life verse." At that graduation, more graduates selected this verse (Jer. 29:11) as their life verse than any other verse.

BABYLON

Babylon was probably the most advanced culture on earth. Herodotus, the Greek historian, says that Babylon was overwhelming in its size and magnitude. The city was built in a square 13 miles long on each side - a total of 169 square miles. Its streets were lined with houses 3-4 stories in height. (Source: *Unger's Bible Dictionary*) The culture was advanced and the city had wonderful attractions. The Hanging Gardens of Babylon built by Nebuchadnezzar was one of the Seven Wonders of the Ancient World. Nebuchadnezzar also erected great temples to Babylonian gods, including his masterpiece - an 8 story ziggurat - the Temple of Bel.

Nebuchadnezzar's palace was equally immaculate. His throne room was lined with enameled brick configured in exquisite geometric designs. Babylon was protected by a double wall which was deemed impregnable. The city was a fortress filled with wealth and luxury. Babylon was the envy of the civilized world.

AMERICA

Today, the United States of America is the world leader in technology and wealth. Considered for decades the richest nation on earth, the United States is protected by the strongest and most powerful military in the world. It is the envy of the civilized world.

The vast majority of American citizens live in a type of luxury and extravagance unparalleled in history or region. The American hunger for possession is exceeded only by its thirst for indulgence. Its primary values emphasize economic success as a goal so that gratification can be purchased and personally experienced. Here are basic principles of American culture regarding lifestyle:

1. Maintain a big house for your luxury and to impress your acquaintances.
2. Entertain yourself (indulgence) with toys, television, video games or with whatever else your heart desires.
3. Find "security" for yourself and your family in what you own and in what you have hoarded.
4. Expend the remainder of your waking hours acquiring wealth to fund (1), (2) and (3).

PRINCIPLE: American culture is reminiscent of Babylon.

GOD'S PEOPLE IN BABYLON

So the question that people of God (Godly people) in a worldly culture must ask is "How much do I partake of the culture? How much does the culture influence me?"

The Jews in Babylon had guidance on this issue. Hundreds of thousands of Jews had been carried into captivity. Jeremiah told them to thrive in the culture in which they lived:

Thus says the Lord of hosts, the God of Israel, to all the exiles whom I have sent into exile from Jerusalem to Babylon, "Build houses and live in them; and plant gardens, and eat their produce. Take wives and become the fathers of sons and daughters, and take wives for your sons and give your daughters to husbands, that they may bear sons and daughters; and multiply there and do not decrease. And seek the welfare of the city where I have sent you into exile, and pray to the Lord on its behalf; for in its welfare you will have welfare." Jer. 29:4-7.

The Jews in Babylon took this word to heart. They prospered in Babylon, establishing strong and growing communities. Some Jews like Daniel and Nehemiah achieved preeminence in the service of the kingdom. The Jews became an important part of the fabric of Babylonian culture.

GOD'S PEOPLE IN AMERICA

Likewise, Christians in America have partaken of its culture. They work in America's commercial enterprises of every type. Many Christians are prosperous executives, financiers, lawyers, entrepeneurs, and developers. They possess wealth, prestige and power, and own opulent houses, cars and entertainment. Christians in America are second to no group in quality of lifestyle, play, and politics. Christians are an important part of the fabric of American culture.

REPROACH

During the time that most Jews were prospering in Babylon, a few Jews remained in Jerusalem. The Lord had promised that Jerusalem, because of its sins, would be made a "curse to all the nations of the earth." Jer. 26:6. The remnant in Jerusalem lived during the "days of its desolation." II Chron. 36:21. These people eked out their livelihood on parched farms and scorched earth. Defenseless to their enemies, they were subjected to the tyranny and cruelty of neighbors that hated them. As Nehemiah was informed, the people who survived the captivity were "in great distress and reproach." Neh. 1:3. What would it take for this reproach to be removed?

> PRINCIPLE: The reproach of the people in Jerusalem was both spiritual and physical.

Our church started a Food Pantry to try to help provide food for needy families. I regularly announced the Food Pantry at Boyz Club, and asked any of the young men to see me if their families needed food. One hot summer evening, at the end of a Boyz Club meeting, eleven year-old Ninh came up to me and pulled on my pants leg. He said, "My family needs food. Can you help us?"

I asked him where he lived. We walked to my car and rode across the street to visit his family. Ninh's family lived in a small apartment with 2 bedrooms and 1 bath.

As we went in the door of the apartment, the first thing that struck me was that the temperature did not change when I walked in from the scorching heat outside. The apartment felt stifling. The apartment was equipped with central air conditioning, but Ninh's family did not have the money to pay for the electricity to run it.

The second thing that struck me was the living room. It was the only living area in the apartment, and it was tiny. But there was a bed set up in the living room with a teenage girl sitting on it. I discovered that a family of seven people lived in these cramped quarters.

I spoke with Ninh's father to gather information about the family's circumstances. Ninh helped to translate his father's broken English. Ninh's father worked a "minimum wage" job, but he had been ill and missed a lot of work. On initial Food Pantry visits, I try to inspect the kitchen to assess the level of need. When I opened the refrigerator door, it was almost empty.

Thankful for our Food Pantry, I delivered food to Ninh's family the next day.

There is desolation in our world today.

DISCIPLESHIP AND WEALTH

Discipleship is a tough word. A disciple is a follower. A disciple of Jesus is a follower of Jesus. The question of what it means to follow Jesus presents a dilemma for American Christians today.

We follow Jesus – the same Jesus who never owned a home, a horse, a plow or even a Porsche. Jesus had no savings. When He owed a tax, he had to extract the money to pay it from the mouth of a fish. Mt. 17:27. Itinerant and unattached, Jesus did not even have a place that he could call "home." "The foxes have holes, and the birds of the air have nests; but the Son of Man has nowhere to lay His head." Mt. 8:20. When He died, Jesus' only possession available for distribution was the clothing off his back. Mt. 27:35. It is this penniless, homeless, and unworldly model that prosperous Christians claim not only to follow, but also to imitate.

The standard of Jesus for the disciples who tried to follow Him was equally strict. "If anyone wishes to come after Me, let him deny himself, and take up his cross daily, and follow Me. For whosoever wishes to save his life shall lose it, but whoever loses his life for My sake, he is the one who will save it." Lk. 9:23-24. When Jesus sent out His disciples for ministry, He told them not to take bread, or a purse, or money – not even an extra change of clothing. Lk. 9:3. The rich young ruler desired to become a disciple of Jesus. Jesus told him to "go and sell all you possess, and give it to the poor, and you shall have treasure in heaven; and come, follow Me." Mk. 10:21. This commandment is consistent with each one of Jesus' teachings about wealth, riches, money and the kingdom of God. Here is Jesus' instruction to His followers: "Sell your possessions, and give to charity." Lk. 12:33.

So the wealthy, landed, filled and "secure" American Christian beholds his model and hears His instructions. What is our response? How do we reconcile our relative wealth with Jesus' words and action? Besides a sense of basic denial supported by self-serving justifications, the response of the typical prosperous Christian is separation. We separate our "Christian life" from our "American life." The American Christian attends church on Sunday and hears the clear teaching of Jesus. Then we spend the rest of the week striving for worldly success. We participate in occasional charitable work, but revel in good "clean" family fun every weekend. We give a little time or money to the poor (maybe even 10%?), but socialize extensively with our equally rich and entertaining friends. We live a schizophrenic life. Our spiritual life is compartmentalized such that it is "just enough" to claim that we have one.

What is the truth? Does the normal prosperous Christian spend his talent acquiring wealth rather than giving it away? Is the bulk of our energy spent on self-indulgence rather than self-sacrifice? Is our time devoted to entertainment rather than to ministry in the kingdom? The shame of the typical American Christian is that he lives just like everyone else in America.

This is the reproach of the American church: It is more influenced by American culture than by the culture of the kingdom of God. Next door live poor, hungry and oppressed people. But comfort and pleasure are more important to us than the needs of our neighbors.

> PRINICIPLE: Many American Christians love themselves more than they love their neighbor.

THE COST OF COMMITMENT

Nehemiah lived in the most advanced culture in the world. Not only was his life in the palace lush, but his job was plush. The cupbearer to the king of Babylon served as a close confidant and adviser to the most important man on earth. It was a powerful and profitable post.

But Nehemiah heard the call of God. He left his comfortable lifestyle to go to one of the most desolate places on earth. Imagine what his friends said: "Let me get this straight, Nehemiah. You are going to leave one of the most coveted jobs in the greatest place on earth to travel 750 miles to a desolate town in a remote, outlying province that you have never seen. What are you thinking?"

> PRINCIPLE: Nehemiah's call required a significant change of lifestyle.

My friend, Goose, is trying to live a sacrificial life based on the teachings of Christ. His work is to minister the Gospel to the needs of the community around him. Goose serves a very poor section of Charlotte. He has a wife and three young children. I had lunch one day with him to hear how the ministry was going. Goose said:

"I haven't been able to take a paycheck for 22 days. I am behind in my tax payments. But how am I supposed to keep the money for myself when the people that I know, and that I am called to love, are hungry and without food?

"My family and I have lost our health insurance coverage. My friends tell me that I am foolish. But earthly security is not a kingdom value. Almost none of the people that I tell about Jesus have insurance coverage. How can I spend money on my health insurance when they have such great needs? I have to rely on the Lord to protect me and my family. That is my witness.

"Right now we have two poor neighborhood children staying with us. We have taken young people into our home before who were physically and sexually abused. My friends tell me that I am stupid because I am exposing my young children to dysfunction

and danger. But I want my children to participate in the gospel – to see it and to experience it. Just the other day, I overheard my little girl and her poor friend from the apartments talking about how they would like to make bracelets and sell them so they could use the money to give food to the poor and tell other people about Jesus.

"I can't live my life according to the values of the world. To me, the gospel is not something that you just say. The gospel is something that you are – something that you live. What good is the gospel if it does not change you? So many people come to the Lord, but it doesn't change how they live or who they are. Jesus calls us to change - to be different than the culture of the world.

"For me, the gospel is my life."

PRINCIPLE: The gospel is our life, not just a belief.

COMMITMENT

The Lord gave Nehemiah a plan. But the plan had an essential component. That component was the people. But the people of Jerusalem had to change their lifestyle and to commit themselves to the work. And every person in Jerusalem was needed. There were not many people in Jerusalem. The plan would work only if all the people of Jerusalem committed to a life of sacrifice to do the work.

When Nehemiah shared his call to build with the people of Jerusalem, he shared it with two groups of people. The first group was the remnant who had lived in desolate Jerusalem during the Babylonian captivity. These citizens of Jerusalem had to give up their jobs and their resources in order to participate in the building of the wall. But that remnant knew that they had to change. They had experienced reproach and shame for many years. They were motivated to build.

The second group had been in Babylon, but they heard the call of God to return to Jerusalem and to rebuild the city. They left their culture in Babylon to do the Lord's work. The group that left Babylon had to give up their lives of ease and prosperity in Babylon to return to a forsaken place. But the call of the Lord on their lives was strong enough for them to leave and to go. This group was also motivated to build. They were willing to sacrifice to fulfill their destiny in the Lord.

> PRINCIPLE: Building the wall required sacrifice by the people who built it.

Both groups were motivated to build the wall. These are the type of people that are needed to build a wall in the community. The people who recognize their condition and the condition of the community around them and are committed to do the work of God. The people who hear the call of the Lord and who are willing to change their lifestyle to fulfill their destiny in Him.

THEY FORGOT

But there is a third group of people: Those who did not build.

Jer. 29:11 says this: "For I know the plans that I have for you," declares the Lord, "plans for welfare and not calamity to give you a future and a hope." But that is a verse taken out of a passage. Here is the full context of the verse:

> For thus says the Lord. "When seventy years have been completed for Babylon, I will visit you and fulfill My good word to you to bring you back to this place. For I know the plans that I have for you," declares the Lord, "plans for welfare and not calamity to give you a future and a hope. Then you will call upon Me and come and pray to Me, and I will listen to you. And you will seek Me and find Me, when you search for Me with all your heart. And I will be found by you," declares the Lord, "and I will restore your fortunes and will gather you from all the nations and from all the places where I have driven you," declares the Lord, "and **I will bring you back to the place from where I sent you into exile.**" Jer. 29:10-14.

Jeremiah told the Jews in Babylon to prosper. They fulfilled that part. They built houses, planted, produced, married and multiplied. But, when the time came to rebuild, He instructed the Jews to come back to Jerusalem and to claim their heritage in the Lord!

But what happened? Most Jews liked the culture of Babylon too well! They forgot to return like Jeremiah told them. They didn't want to leave their wealth; the journey was extremely difficult; and the work was too harsh. The sacrifice was too much. They were not willing to change their lifestyle to obey the Lord.

"The whole number of the exiles that chose to remain [in Babylon] was probably about **six times** the number of those who returned." (Source: Easton's Bible Dictionary). The failure of so many exiles to return from Babylon was the reason only a few – a remnant – were left to do the work of the Lord in Jerusalem. "The city was large and spacious and the people in it were few." Neh. 7:4. For most of those in exile in Babylon, to leave the homes they had built; to leave the culture and lifestyle they were experiencing; to make that long and arduous journey to return to a broken down city - it simply was not worth it.

The same failure is true of American Christians today. To give up their comfort; to change their lifestyle; and to journey to unsafe and unsavory places to interact with strange persons – even in their own cities; it simply isn't worth it. The sacrifice is too much. They are not willing to change their lifestyle to obey the Lord.

But the ones who do – these are precious comrades. They recognize their own condition. They see the condition of the community around them. They are willing to change in order to follow and imitate their Lord. They commit to His work. They sacrifice time, money, comfort, and security in order to do His will. These true disciples are the ones who affirm like those in Jerusalem: "Let us arise and build." Neh. 2:18.

HERITAGE

What did the few Jews who obeyed Jeremiah, left their homes in Babylon, and journeyed to Jerusalem, receive? Their heritage in the Lord. Their heritage in Jerusalem. The plans that the Lord had for them - plans for a future and a hope.

The Jews that stayed in the comfort of Babylon and did not return as Jeremiah told them, what did they exchange for that comfort? They forfeited their heritage in the Lord. They lost their heritage in Jerusalem.

The Lord has a heritage for His people today. It is a heritage that God intends his people to reach out and claim through their work in Him. Ps. 111:6 says "He has made known to His people the power of His works, In giving them the heritage of the nations."

Charles Spurgeon expounds on this verse in his commentary, <u>The Treasury of David</u>:

"He hath shewed his people the power of his works." They have seen what he is able to do and what force he is prepared to put forth on their behalf. This power Israel saw in physical works, and we in spiritual wonders, for we behold the matchless energy of the Holy Ghost and feel it in our own souls. In times of dire distress the Lord has put forth such energy of grace that we have been astonished at his power; and this was part of his intent in bringing us into such conditions that he might reveal to us the arm of his strength. Could we ever have known it so well if we had not been in pressing need of his help? We may well turn this verse into a prayer and ask to see more and more the power of the Lord at work among us in these latter days. "O Lord, let us now see how mightily thou canst work in the saving of sinners and in preserving and delivering thine own people." *"That he may give them the heritage of the heathen."* He put forth all his power to drive out the Canaanites and bring in his people. Even thus may it please his infinite wisdom to give to his church the heathen for her inheritance in the name of Jesus. Nothing but great power can effect this, but it will surely be accomplished in due season.

The heritage that the Lord intends for His people today is to bring the nations to Him. To save sinners so that they, too, become disciples and followers of Him. The peoples are our inheritance.

Here is the fundamental choice: Are we willing to forsake the pleasures of our Babylon to claim our heritage in the Lord? It takes hard work together as a community to build a wall. Are we willing to leave our Babylon in order to bring nations to the Lord? Is obedience to the Lord's clear commands to make disciples that important to us?

How important is our heritage in the Lord? Does it mean enough to us to forsake our wonderful American culture?

This choice is vital, and it has eternal consequence. Nehemiah did not have many resources, but he did have motivated people who were committed to the work.

What is your choice?

MEDITATION: "A rich man's wealth is his strong city, And like a high wall in his imagination." Prov. 18:11

1. To what extent is your life and your time invested in your possessions?

2. Have you ever felt a conviction that your possessions and lifestyle reflect the values of worldly culture rather than Jesus' example?

3. If so, what action did you take in response to that conviction?

4. Is there a difference between believing the gospel and living the gospel?

5. Describe your heritage in the Lord at this present time.

REVIEW:

1. American culture is reminiscent of Babylon.

2. What it means to follow Jesus presents a dilemma for the typical American Christian today.

3. The reproach of the American church is that it is influenced more by American culture than by the culture of the kingdom.

4. Many American Christians love themselves more than they love their neighbor.

5. Nehemiah's call required a significant change of lifestyle.

6. The gospel is our life, not just a belief.

7. Building the wall required sacrifice by the people who built it.

8. Most Jews in Babylon were not willing to leave their luxury to build in Jerusalem.

9. The Jews who returned from Babylon claimed their heritage in the Lord.

10. The heritage of the saints is the nations of the earth.

RESOURCE #1: STEPS TO A PLAN

1. Through prayer, establish God as your Source. Don't leave Him. He will not leave you.

2. Pursue corporate call. Seek God regarding which community (or area) to impact.

3. Assume responsibility for that community beginning with confession, repentance and intercession.

4. Wait until the Lord empowers you to act. At the point of empowerment, act immediately.

5. Survey the community for issues, needs and resources.

6. Prayer walk regularly through the community.

7. Pray for a plan for the community.

8. Pray for people committed to the work who will join you.

9. Communicate the plan to persons who might commit to the work.

10. Commit personally and corporately to the change of lifestyle required to do the work of building in the community.

RESOURCE #2 – OUTREACH STRATEGIES, MINISTRIES AND EVENTS

[This resource is a compilation of some outreach ideas. The list is far from exhaustive since approaches and methods are as limitless as people and culture. The purpose of this resource is to describe some options for ministry to your community, and through its descriptions, to enhance planning and strategies for outreach. Survey your community, then pray and brainstorm about the approaches and methods that God wants you to use.]

(Parentheses indicate ministries in our area that have conducted the ministry indicated.)

1. **SPIRITUAL**

Children's Clubs – A children's club welcomes boys and girls ages 4-12 for games, snacks, songs, and Bible stories told in age and gender appropriate groups. (Good Shepherd Club)

Youth Clubs – These clubs (many are segregated by gender) include youth from ages 10-18, many of them formerly children's club members. Events include sports or games, followed by a meeting with worship and Biblical teaching. Use of a small group format for meetings offers the opportunity to train youth leaders in leading groups, prayer and Bible study. (Boyz Club and Girlz Club)

Bible Study – These weekly Bible studies are deeper and more advanced studies for young adults and adults, especially those youth that age out of youth clubs. A primary focus of these studies is growth in faith, in Christian character, and in Christian disciplines, along with leadership training for new generations of urban ministers and missionaries. (Monday Night Bible Study)

Retreats – Many clubs and bible studies sponsor weekend retreats for their members, usually at the beach, mountains or a camp. The retreats are a great tool for focused instruction in accordance with the "theme" of the weekend. The retreats also enhance relationship building. For inner city and refugee families, the experience of a nonurban environment is renewing and often horizon expanding. (Boyz Club Retreat)

Church Participation/Membership – The invitation to families and youth to attend church services or youth group meetings is an opportunity to experience and to participate in Body life.

Prayer Walking – Prayer walking takes prayer to the streets and neighborhoods of communities in which ministry occurs. Prayer is the foundation of discipleship and ministry. But prayer walking allows the disciple to experience the area of ministry and to learn its needs, and to interact with persons in the community that they meet along the way.

Vacation Bible School – This youth event can be held at a church, or at a location in the community of ministry. VBS is a good event to offer fun, fellowship and teaching, while initiating or developing relationships with participants. (Good Shepherd VBS)

Ethnic Congregations – Many established churches allow sister churches with a specific ethnic composition to use their facilities. Not only is the use of a meeting facility a blessing to the other churches, but the congregations have the opportunity to collaborate in events together. Many ethnic churches have been founded with help from urban ministries. (Vietnamese, Montagnard, Hispanic, Nepali, Burmese and Congolese Churches)

2. **EDUCATION**

English As a Second Language (ESL) – This class helps recent arrivals in America learn English. It is a great means of developing relationship with ESL students, and can incorporate Biblical teaching or values in its curriculum. (Catholic Charities)

After School – This program for students provides tutoring on a daily basis. Devotions, teaching, sharing, and even meals (nutrition) occur regularly, and the frequent relational interaction is a means of great influence. (Good Shepherd After School, Focus Academy)

Tutoring – Tutoring can occur weekly or more often after school as an educational supplement.

Tutoring meets an educational need while developing relationships. Tutoring can be conducted in partnership with schools, public agencies, or even libraries. (Boyz Club Tutoring)

Driver's License//Application for Government Assistance – This ministry assists refugee and poor families in gaining licensure or other program qualification necessary to survive in our society.

Topical Classes – Classes in areas of life function such as parenting, money management, cooking, nutrition, hygiene, cleaning, and marriage offer opportunities for education, assistance and relationship. (Financial Peace University)

Community School – Community schools provide a secure environment for the education of youth. The daily interaction is effective in teaching, discipleship and building character in the lives of the students. A community school is the difference between educational success and educational failure for many students. (One7 Academy)

College – Financial assistance, scholarships and guidance inspire urban youth to gain admittance to college, to attend, and to graduate. Some colleges are willing to partner with urban programs.

3. **PHYSICAL NEEDS**

Food Ministry – This ministry distributes food to families that need it. Our model operates through advocates for each needy family. The advocate visits the family and qualifies the need. The advocate then picks up the food and delivers it to the family on a regular basis. (Commonwealth Food Bank//Angel Food Ministries)

Clothing Ministry – This ministry collects new and slightly used clothing and then distributes it to families that need it. As part of sports ministry, we often distribute shoes and sports gear to the youth. (Clothes Closet)

Community Garden – A large garden plot is fenced and divided into small parcels. Different families "rent" those parcels for a nominal fee and grow gardens in each one. A community garden is a great way to offer green space for gardens in an urban environment. Sharing of the produce occurs regularly.

Day Care – Day care offered at reduced cost (or a sliding scale) assists working parents. Day care is an opportunity to teach and influence young lives.

Transportation – Transportation for daily needs such as shopping or for church events affords the opportunity to relate and to share. Our neighborhood bus stops look like grocery cart rodeos due to the number of residents who don't have rides to the grocery store.

Legal Assistance – Assistance for families with legal needs helps them negotiate a system that is complex enough without the challenge of linguistic barriers. Many poor families need an advocate to protect them from injustice.

Health Care – Clinics and health care classes assist families with pressing health or dental needs.

Thrift Store – "One man's junk is another man's treasure." A thrift store offers needed items at low prices using donations from the community and a little imagination.

Christmas – Christmas is a wonderful time to bless poor families with food, money and gifts. Angel Tree allows church members to buy gifts or to donate money to a specific child or family. The Christmas Gift Store allows poor families to purchase Christmas gifts at greatly reduced prices. (Angel Tree//Nexus Christmas Gift Store).

Visitation – Participants in this ministry visit friends and acquaintances in the community. Through regular visitation, friendships are cultivated, sharing occurs, and needs are discerned so they can be met. One such ministry matches an outreach family with a needy family. The outreach family commits to visit its assigned family regularly (weekly). (Fruitful Friends)

Employment – Employment assistance can be given through a job resource center or a job placement center. Another approach is to produce and to market goods in an indigenous cottage industry. Many cultures produce marketable weaving, art, clothing, cooking or crafts. (Project 658)

Homeless Ministry – From regular meals to housing to visitation, homeless ministry can meet needs of the homeless and offer hope for recovery. Because of the dysfunction, mental illness and addictions that often accompany homelessness, effective homeless ministry is time consuming, stressful and demanding. (Hoskins Park Ministries)

4. **RECREATIONAL OUTLETS**

Worship/Arts Programs – This ministry offers singing, dancing or other arts classes and instruction to impoverished youth and/or their families. (Dancing Together//Graffitti Art)

Field Trips – Clubs or groups visit a local attraction such as a park, museum, botanical garden or historical site. The trip provides a relief from "urban doldrums" and a chance to interact through friendship ministry.

Sports Teams – Sports teams or leagues offer the opportunity not only for recreation, but to grow and learn about life through teaching, teamwork and sportsmanlike competition. Coaching is a position of authority that is a means of great influence due to frequent interaction. In many ways, sports training and competition parallel life within a structured setting. (One7 Ministries, MAI - Urban Eagles)

Block Parties – Block parties can be community-wide events that offer music, food, games, crafts, dance or even carnival rides for the neighborhood. Block parties can bring different ethnicities and socioeconomic classes together in a celebration of life. A smaller variation of a block party is a cook-out where we set up a grill and provide food, drinks and fellowship. (Fall

Fest//Spring Fling)

Holiday Parties – Holiday parties can offer games, gifts, food and fellowship, while sharing the story of the occasion (such as Christmas or Easter) through plays or teaching stations. (Eyewitnesses to Easter)

Christian Camps – Weekend or weeklong camps offer young people a chance to recreate, fellowship, experience new activities, and grow in faith. The camps can focus on an activity such as sports or dance, or can offer multiple activities. (Urban Eagles Soccer Camp//LHCC - Learning Help Centers of Charlotte//Summer Christian camps).

Concerts/Movies – Offering free concerts or movies for a community provides wholesome entertainment along with the opportunity to connect, share, fellowship and laugh together.

Multi-cultural Banquets/Festivals – A gathering of different cultures to eat together and share cultural cuisine, dance, music or stories helps bring cultures together and provides a foundation for friendship and trust. (International Banquet)

5. **TRAINING**

Internships – The most effective way of learning ministry is doing it side by side with a caring and experienced minister. Interns provide valuable assistance to ministries while acquiring knowledge, skill and ability. (One7 Internships, MAI – Urban Eagles Residency)

Leadership Retreats – Retreats with young (or older) leaders offer the opportunity to teach leadership principles and to exchange ideas about ministry, vision, and call. (Boyz Club Leadership Retreat)

Ministry Training Trips – Trips to do urban ministry in other areas provide the opportunity for potential leaders to conduct ministry outreaches. (One7 Chicago)

Service Projects/Trips – Instilling the value of service to the poor and needy is key to spiritual growth and training. Performing service projects for one day or one week is a healthy and beneficial activity for urban youth and leaders. (Love, Inc.//One7 Mission Lin Garden//Boyz Club Service Trip)

6. **INCARNATIONAL PRESENCE**

Apartment – Renting an apartment in the community itself for ministry use, or for residences for committed urban ministers, is a great way to impact the community. Presence is an important component of ministry. (Good Shepherd Apartment//Apartment Life//Urban Eagles)

Adoption/Foster Care – Parenting may be the highest level of discipleship. Christians who adopt needy children or who provide foster care sacrifice their lives and their homes to love those in greatest need.

Resource Office – A resource office located in the community can assist its residents with referrals, forms and resources for many needs and opportunities. (Refugee Support Services)

Community Center//Fields – A community center for recreation, education and meetings provides a valuable outlet for young and old alike in the area, along with the occasion to interact with its residents.

Multi-family Housing//Group Homes – Providing housing on a reduced basis (or sliding scale) assists persons who are below the poverty line or who have other needs to live, to function, and hopefully to recover.

SECTION TWO:
BODY WORK –
EXECUTING THE PLAN

LESSON EIGHT - MOTIVATION

My friend was enthusiastic. He was attending a megachurch that was growing rapidly. "We put in 500 more seats a couple of months ago" he said, "and now those seats are full!"

I thought for a minute. "That sounds great!" I replied. "I guess that growth is a good thing, and I am sure that the gospel is being preached. Not everyone that attends church though is a follower of Jesus. In fact, many people who attend church aren't fruitful in their Christian lives."

My friend agreed.

I continued. "For me, one of the keys is task-based small groups. Small groups are a good thing. But if the small groups aren't active in productive ministry, they exist as a world unto themselves. A group needs to reach out in ministry to become alive."

It was as if a light went on. "That's right!" my friend affirmed, pumping his fist as he said it. "We need a purpose to exist!"

"It's kind of like the idea of quest. A common quest to fulfill together in establishing the kingdom!"

My friend stopped. "Man!" he almost shouted. "I have been in a small group for 15 years. We have the same 8 people. And we meet and we help each other to grow, but we don't do anything! We aren't alive!"

"If you don't produce fruit, you may spiritually be dead or dying."

"No, we aren't dead."

"But you aren't alive."

"No, we aren't alive."

"You aren't dead and you aren't alive. You are the living dead. You are the Christian zombies!"

My friend turned to me. "You're right. That is what we are – Christian zombies!"

Not dead but not alive. Christian zombies. People that know the urgency of the gospel. People that sit and hear eloquent preaching week after week about call to work in the Kingdom.

But for some reason, it is not enough to prompt action. Maybe it's "I can't do it!" (Fear); or "I won't do it!" (Pride); or "I'm too busy!" (Pleasure). Whatever the excuse, Christian zombies live all around us.

How do we engage people of faith who are mired in worldly culture to join in the work?

STEP #1 – VISION CASTING

"Then I said to them, 'You see the bad situation we are in, that Jerusalem is desolate and its gates burned by fire. Come, let us rebuild the wall of Jerusalem that we may no longer be a reproach.' And I told them how the hand of my God had been favorable to me, and also about the king's words which he had spoken to me. Then they said, 'Let us arise and build.' So they put their hands to the good work." Neh. 2:17-18.

First, Nehemiah communicated his plan to the people. He showed them their plight. The people were in reproach – a reproach not unlike that of the Christian zombie. Nehemiah described the condition of the community around them. He described its desolation.

Then Nehemiah laid out his plan. He presented a solution to the problem.

> PRINCIPLE: Vision casting describes both the problem and the solution.

But Nehemiah did not present just *a* solution. Nehemiah presented *God's* solution. "I told them how the hand of my God had been favorable to me..." Nehemiah cast a vision and assured the people "The Lord is in it!"

> PRINCIPLE: Effective vision casting reveals the hand of the Lord in the work.

A plan is important. But the plan will fail unless the Lord is the Source of the plan. The hand of the Lord must be in the work.

Workers formed into task-based small groups or teams are also important. But they will still fail – unless they know they are called by God to do the work. The call of the Lord will sustain them in times when there is nothing else to stand on. Call must be communicated and be defined.

STEP #2 – INVITATION

Love crosses lines. A selfish person expects others to enter his world and to see things his way. In fact, he is offended when they do not. But love leaves its own world – its comfort, its possessions and its expectations, to reach across the divide and enter the world of another. Love looks beyond its own perceptions in order to understand the perceptions of another.

That is the difference between attractional ministry and missional ministry. Attractional ministry expects the other person leave his world and to enter into your world. Missional ministry goes to that person and enters his world in order to show that person love, to meet his needs, and to minister truth to him. Missional ministry enters the world of the other person in order to tell him about the kingdom.

There are settings in which attractional ministry is appropriate and effective. But in the culture of our world today, missional ministry is necessary. Love compels us to cross a line into another person's world if for no other reason than to show him love.

> Love crosses lines.

But crossing lines is uncomfortable. It implies that we are forced to leave our selfish world and sacrifice our security. How do we encourage other believers to cross lines and to join the work?

"And I also applied myself to the work on this wall..." Neh. 5:16

Through the years, we have used many methods of asking for volunteers to join the work. We made presentations; we put needs in the church bulletin; and we shared stories

about the work to encourage others to join it. These efforts had limited success.

Here is our most effective way to recruit workers: A minister who is active doing the work invites an interested person to come and work beside him. A personal invitation directed to the right person does wonders.

Here is what I do: I make a connection with a person that is a potential worker. I describe what we are doing and invite him to come and see it for himself. Many people won't come. But if he comes once, I share with him a little more about our vision. Then I see if he comes back. Many don't come back. But if he starts coming regularly, I invite him to lunch.

At lunch, I listen. I listen to what he is doing. I listen to his background, and I listen to his heart. I then share my heart with him. The goal is to discern if the Lord is calling him to this work.

If the Lord is calling him to the work, I invite him to do the work of the ministry together. If that person shows faithfulness to that call, I make it a point to connect with him regularly, and to eat lunch with him routinely. I help him grow in ministry, and he helps me grow as well.

Through the years, I have eaten many lunches with many workers. Sometimes it lasts for a season. And sometimes it lasts for years.

THE CALL (Book One – Functional) says "It is difficult to teach what you have not experienced." Personal experience in an area of ministry uniquely equips a person to teach about it. To draw workers into a ministry, I would add this principle: It is difficult to draw workers to a ministry if you yourself are not doing it.

Many times that is the difficulty of a call to action from the pulpit. The preacher needs to present himself as a working example of the ministry he is espousing, and – even better - to offer personal assistance to the responsive hearer.

Invitation by an active minister eliminates excuses.

To "I can't do it" - you say, "Why not? I do it."

To "I'm too busy" – you say, "I used to think that as well, but here I am doing it."

To "I won't do it" – you say, "Here, let me go with you. That is easier."

"And Jesus turned, and beheld them following, and said to them, 'What do you seek?' And they said to Him, 'Rabbi (which translated means Teacher), where are You staying?' He said to them, '**Come, and you will see.**' They came therefore and saw where He was staying; and they stayed with Him that day, for it was about the tenth hour." Jn. 1:38-39.

> PRINCIPLE: It is difficult to draw workers to a ministry if you yourself are not doing it.

Don't despair if it takes time for workers to come. Be faithful to the call that the Lord has in your life. Do the work of ministry. But keep your eye open for others that might join you. Invite them in and then give them room to operate in the ministry.

A team is not built in a day. It is a gradual process into which the Lord wondrously weaves many lives – in His time and by His design.

STEP #3 – ENCOURAGE RESPONSIBILITY

I have a deep appreciation for my friend, John. I call him "evangelist John." He has a heart to share the gospel.

John has an unusual talent. John is a "graffiti artist." It sounds strange, but it is effective in the inner city. John puts down a piece of plywood in the neighborhood, and with a few cans of spray paint, he creates devotional masterpieces.

It always gathers a crowd. Then John asks a few of the young spectators if they would like to learn how to do it. Together they create the masterpieces. Before long, John has made a few friends and shared the gospel of Jesus Christ in the process.

When a new worker of good reputation and character comes into the ministry, as soon as feasible, encourage and allow him (or her) to take responsibility in the ministry. Give him room to do so.

When a new person comes, we immediately look for his gifts or talents. We try to discern what that person can add to the ministry, and where he can fit. My friend, John, has an unusual gift, but it is effective in the areas that we minister.

Here is how responsibility helps a new worker develop:

1. <u>You Strengthen</u> - Taking responsibility helps strengthen your gifts. Exercising your gift strengthens the gift; not using your gift causes the gift to atrophy.

I have a "milking muscle" in my forearms. The hand action of milking a cow requires a person to use the muscles in their forearm. My milking muscle is weak now, but it used to be very strong. When I was young, I milked a cow every night. When I exercised my milking gift, it developed hard and bulging milking muscles. But I haven't used that milking gift in a long time and those milking muscles are weak. But I can stir up that milking gift again and exercise those milking muscles. It would be difficult and painful for the first few nights, but soon my milking muscles would be strong and bulging once again.

Our gifts are like muscles. They need to be exercised to strengthen and grow, and they need connection with other gifts in order to work well. Each of us has gifts from God that we can use to build the wall. Those gifts will grow as we take our place in the building. "Do not neglect the spiritual gift within you, which was bestowed upon you through prophetic utterance with the laying on of hands by the presbytery. Take pains with these things; be absorbed in them, so that your progress may be evident to all." I Tim. 4:14-15

2. <u>You Learn</u> - The people of Jerusalem had to learn on the job. The people may not have been builders at the beginning of the work, but they probably could do a little rock work by the end of it. We learn ministry by doing it. Instruction imparts knowledge. Training imparts the application of that knowledge. Instruction requires listening. Training requires doing.

The training of workers is vital.

> PRINCIPLE: Training in the ministry so it can be duplicated in another place and time is always a primary goal of ministry.

I am always looking for opportunities to advance new workers. Training side by side is an effective method.

Vit is one of our Boyz Club youth leaders. After he prepared and shared a Bible lesson at our small group Monday night Bible study a few times, I asked Vit to consider sharing a lesson at the much larger Boyz Club and conducting the meeting. Vit was hesitant and uncertain. He had never done it before. But I encouraged him to do it and he agreed.

Vit led the worship the next week, and spoke to the group. At times he seemed unsure of himself, but he shared some good things and he made it through the lesson.

Vit was blessed, and I was blessed.

Did Vit lead that Boyz Club meeting as well as I could have? Probably not. But that is not the point. The point is this: One day, Vit will do it better than I can. That is my goal.

Training implies that you allow workers to perform at their level of expertise. Did the people building the wall make mistakes? Of course they did. But the work would not have occurred if the people had allowed fear of mistakes to stop them. Don't be afraid to undertake what the Lord has for you and for others!

3. <u>You Grow and Mature</u> - Taking responsibility yields growth. There was a small group of young men that met at my house for Bible study –Monday night Bible study. The time came for them to move from instruction into training. Here is what I shared with them about responsibility at that time:

"Do you want to mature in the Lord? Do you want to grow in ministry? Then take responsibility in the Lord's work. When you begin doing the Lord's work, you will learn as much or more than you will teach.

"Guys, it is like becoming a parent. Every parent is an amateur. When I became a parent, I thought that I was the teacher, and my children were the learners. I thought I was grown, and my children were growing. I thought that I was the giver, and my children were the recipients. I was wrong.

"One day it dawned upon me that I learned as much from being a parent as my children learned. I realized that I grew as much from being a parent as my children grew. I benefitted as much from being a parent as my children benefitted from being my child.

"It is the same in the Kingdom of God. I can not express the impact of my work on me. Ministry - real ministry - not only causes me to survive. It causes me to thrive."

> PRINCIPLE: Taking responsibility helps to strengthen the disciple and it gives him an opportunity to learn and to grow into maturity.

Growth leads to maturity. As you take responsibility, you mature. What does a mature Christian do? A mature Christian bears fruit. The biblical test for discipleship is the fruit that you bear. The hallmark of a mature Christian is fruitfulness. "By this is My Father glorified, that you bear much fruit, and so prove to be My disciples." Jn. 15:8

And a fruitful Christian is alive. He is no longer a zombie.

MEDITATION: "For he said to Judah, 'Let us build these cities and surround them with walls and towers, gates and bars. The land is still ours; because we have sought the Lord our God; we have sought Him, and He has given us rest on every side.' So they built and prospered." II Chron. 14:7.

1. How important is the assurance that the Lord is in the work to be undertaken?

2. How can we know that the Lord is in the work?

3. Have you ever been encouraged to join a work? If so, how did that invitation occur?

4. What are some keys to assimilating new workers into a work?

REVIEW:

1. Vision casting describes both the problem and the solution.

2. Effective vision casting reveals the hand of the Lord in the work.

3. Love crosses lines.

4. The most effective recruitment is when a minister who is active doing the work invites an interested person to come and work beside him.

5. It is difficult to draw workers to a ministry if you yourself are not doing it.

6. Training in the ministry so it can be duplicated in another place and time is always a primary goal of ministry.

7. Taking responsibility helps to strengthen the disciple, and it gives him an opportunity to learn and to grow into maturity.

LESSON NINE - THE BUILDERS

"Then Eliashib the high priest arose with his brothers the priests and built the Sheep Gate..." Neh. 3:1

After years of outreach to refugee and inner city youth, I had a problem. Week after week, I was out on the soccer field surrounded by dozens of young people who lived in the inner city. But I felt alone. No one else seemed to understand the same vision for the ministry or to want to help with the soccer on a consistent basis. I felt that I was doing sports ministry by myself. As that perception grew, I began to feel sorry for myself.

After another afternoon alone on the soccer field, I felt pretty low. I went home and sat down. I decided to write the names of friends and acquaintances that had helped the ministry at some point.

First, I thought of our soccer camps. Bethany, Elisha, and Rachel from my church had volunteered to prepare and bring food for the campers one year. I wrote down their names.

Next, I thought of the recreational league teams sponsored by my church that had refugee children on them. Rob, Stephen, Kenny, Heidi and Mike had coached those teams, and – bless her heart – Debbie had organized those teams for years. I wrote down their names.

Then, I thought of the Charlotte Eagles Soccer Club. They had conducted clinics at the apartments and shared with the youth. They had provided free tickets to bring the youth to the games. I wrote down more names.

Before long, my list was over 20 names. My perception that I had been doing the ministry alone was simply wrong. I had to repent.

Now, years later, I have some fantastic ministry partners. We work together. Many coworkers have a full time job like I do. They sacrifice their spare time to do ministry. They are there week after week – doing tutoring on Mondays, helping with Boyz Club on Wednesdays, or sacrificing their Saturdays to deliver food to needy families.

Other coworkers spend full time in ministry. They devote far more time to the

ministry than I do – expanding and fulfilling the vision to build in our communities.

Let me tell you something: I appreciate my coworkers. They are great teammates. I try to encourage them in their work and their sacrifice. And I thank them for being there.

The description of who built the wall in Nehemiah is just as important to the work as the method of building it. Chapter 3 of the book of Nehemiah tells us who built the wall, and which section they built under Nehemiah's plan. This description is very important because it gives us insight into the nature and personality of the people of Jerusalem who performed this great work. Here are some of the builders listed in Nehemiah 3:

1. Eliashib, the high priest, built and his brothers, the priests (Neh. 3:1). Isn't the high priest supposed to be in the temple ministering to God? Isn't he consecrated to serve in the temple area, not to be out getting his hands dirty? Where in the law of Moses does it tell the high priest to go build a wall? Building a wall is not his call or his vocation. But there the priests were...clothes dirty...faces sweaty...working.
2. There weren't many professional builders. The men who built had a variety of occupations such as salesmen (merchants) (Neh. 3:32), goldsmiths, and perfumers (Neh. 3:8). (Even if the wall wasn't strong, it at least smelled good.)
3. Ruling officials built (Neh. 3:14-16). The rulers of the district of Beth-haccherem; of the district of Mizpah; and of half the district of Beth-zur built. These men were officials used to governing. They were accustomed to others doing the work. But there they were, building a wall. The work was that important.
4. Shallum was another ruler - the official in charge of half the district of Jerusalem. He was outside working and who was building with him? Not builders nor soldiers nor servants. Women were building. And not just women, they were young women – Shallum's own daughters (Neh 3:12). Neither gender nor age is a barrier to serving the Lord. Any person, young or old, who has faith and who practices conscientious obedience to the Lord can be used of God. "But the Lord said to me, 'Do not say 'I am a youth,' because everywhere I send you, you shall go, and all that I command you, you shall speak.'" Jer. 1:7.
5. Many people were building sections of the wall just outside their homes in their own

backyards (Neh. 3:21-23). They built in their home communities.

6. Outsiders came to build - men from Jericho (3:2), Tekoa (Neh. 3:5 and 3:27), Gibeon and Mizpah (Neh. 3:7), and Zanoah (Neh. 3:13). These men lived outside Jerusalem and some of them were not even Hebrews, but they were needed for the work. Maybe they wanted to participate in the work that God had ordained. Maybe they realized that God's presence and authority in Jerusalem would impact their own lives and maybe even expand to their own cities.

7. The Nethinim built. The Nethinim were a special group of temple servants. (Neh. 3:26). They were common laborers who performed menial tasks in the temple. They did not have priestly designation or ordination. But their labor was needed.

8. There was another specific person noted. Baruch built. We don't know much about Baruch, but the list of builders describes Baruch differently than any other person. It says Baruch built "zealously." Neh. 3:20. The encouragement of an enthusiastic worker should be valued and noted.

This group of builders is diverse. It cuts across distinctions based on social standing, ethnicity, gender, age, and occupation. In Jerusalem, the title of "builder" was a very inclusive concept.

> PRINCIPLE: The people that built the wall were diverse in gift, occupation, age and status.

Here are some insights from the list of builders in Nehemiah 3 about the persons and ministries needed to bring the kingdom of God to a community:

CONSISTENCY

A. How committed were the people to the work?

"Then they said, 'Let us arise and build.' So they put their hands to the good work." Neh. 2:18.

The people of Jerusalem committed to the work. The people did not allow their daily jobs to keep them from their work on the wall. Kingdom ministry is hard work. It isn't "wave the magic wand and the people will be blessed." Impactful ministry is time consuming, self-sacrificial, tiring, patience testing, inconvenient, risky, frustrating, intense, draining, full bore, callous on hands and knees work.

We don't just put in a couple of hours a week and then consider the job done. That is neither devotion to ministry nor devotion to the Lord. Paul reminded the church of his efforts: "For you recall, brethren, our labor and hardship, how working night and day so as not to be a burden to any of you, we proclaimed to you the gospel of God." I Thes. 2:9.

Consistency is a key. The impoverished people that we reach are subjected to abject lies, broken promises, intemperate conduct, dissolute lifestyles and shattering abuse. Inconsistency is a hallmark of their lives. A kingdom minister that demonstrates a Godly alternative of consistent presence, loving care and kept promises presents an epiphany for them - and starkly contrasts with many of their parents and peers. It is like an oasis of clear, fresh water in a withering desert.

> PRINCIPLE: Consistent kingdom work reflects the love of God.

The days of the part-time Christian are over. The part-time Christian attends church on Sunday morning. But in all other respects, he partakes of the culture of the world rather than working in ministry. During the week, the part-time Christian labors in worldly commerce, and devotes his spare time to play and to indulge. The part-time Christian performs his weekly religious duty, but fundamentally uses his time, resources, and energy to serve his own interests. He has fused his religion and the culture of the world around him.

The part-time Christian attends a part-time church. A part-time church accommodates the lifestyle of the part-time Christian. The part-time church devotes its time, resources, and facilities to a Sunday morning service. The Sunday morning meeting is that church's primary function and focus. There is so much emphasis on Sunday morning that precious little energy remains for ministry elsewhere. Church leadership tells members of the part-time church that "serving the Lord" means tasks that contribute to the Sunday morning operation - nursery helper, usher, choir member, parking lot attendant or acolyte. Sermons in the part-time church emphasize the need to attend church regularly; the need to be on time; the need to give to the church; and the need to bring a guest so the guest can participate in the church's culture and give to the church as well. The Sunday morning presentation dominates weekly staff meetings – both the question of its production, and the question of how the church can perform it better in order to draw more people.

I had lunch with my coworker, David, this week. David works hard in the ministry in the community. On this day though, he was little frustrated.

"I don't understand my Christian friends. They say that they like and admire the ministry that I am doing. They say that they should be doing the same thing. I encourage them 'Why don't you?'

"But then they respond 'No, I can't. I don't have the ability to do it.'

"I say 'If I can do it, then you can do it. It isn't a matter of ability.' But they just shake their heads and walk off. It isn't that they can't do it. They won't do it. They are too involved in work, their lifestyle or their entertainment. It's as if there is a disconnect between what they believe and what they do.

"I have the same frustration with my pastor. He says that he supports me in my ministry, and I appreciate that support. I tell him that our church should be committed to the ministry as a body.

"Just think what the whole church could do if it was committed to the ministry as a church. Shouldn't a pastor have a vision for ministry for the whole body, and not just for individual members?"

The healthy fulltime church equips its members to exercise their spiritual gifts, encourages and assists in discernment of God's call on their lives, and then releases the members to minister in their community throughout the week - week in and week out. When that Body gathers, it is for celebration of the Lord and His work. The members – many of whom work but devote their spare time to ministry and outreach - report on the work of the Lord in their lives and in the lives of others. Corporate prayer focuses on worship, thanksgiving and the needs of the ongoing work of the Lord. Acts 4:23-31. Those meetings fulfill the Biblical purpose of Christian assembly. They encourage the members of the body, and they stimulate those members to love and to good works. Heb. 10:23-25.

> The days of the part-time Christian are over.

The days of the part-time Christian are over. They are not over because I say so. They are over because the Lord has ordained it. Some part-time Christians will repent and change their lifestyle. They will be blessed for it both in this world and in the world to come. Others will find the fence too uncomfortable to straddle – and they will be forced to choose. The Lord will bring it about.

PREEMINENCE

B. <u>Who was the most important person in this work?</u>

Who was the most important person in this work? The high priest or the temple servant? The official in charge of the whole district of Mizpah, or Shallum's youngest daughter? The goldsmith or the perfumer? Maybe it was Baruch or the Philistine from Gibeon?

I am highly appreciative of Bailey. Bailey has worked with us at Boyz Club for years. When you first meet Bailey, he seems a little strange. In fact, Bailey seems a little "spacey." When you say something to Bailey, there is a pause – as if it takes a moment or two for the words to register. Bailey has a wry sense of humor, and his response is often offbeat.

But Bailey is consistent and dependable. God has called him to the Boyz Club ministry, and he is there every week. He picks up a group of young men and brings them to the meeting. Bailey is a hard worker. He undertakes any task that needs to be done.

What I like about Bailey is his attitude. Sometimes he makes a mistake or he realizes a shortcoming. Here is his response: "Man, I just want learn how to do this ministry that God has called us to do." I have heard Bailey say that a number of times. And Bailey has

grown – both in the Lord and in ministry.

Bailey is the type of guy that I want beside me as I am building on the wall.

Who was the most important builder on the wall? No one person was most important. Every single person was deemed important because every section of the wall was important. In this work of wall building, every person was important because if his section failed, the wall was breached. Each and every person was vital to the task.

> PRINCIPLE: Every single builder was important to the work.

That being said, there was leadership among the builders. The first verse of Nehemiah 3 tells us that the religious officials (high priests and priests) were vested in this work. They personally worked on the wall. Pastor, reverend, minister, bishop, elder, priest, deacon – whatever title a church leader may have – he is essential for the work. Church leaders provide so much - guidance, pastoral care, training, and protection from doctrinal deception.

Many pastors are heavily focused on "in reach." They are occupied (and burdened) with care of the flock. But the church (which is the people) needs both body life and outreach to the community around it. Body life and outreach feed each other. Both are necessary for a healthy body. Imbalance in either area is detrimental and injurious. [See <u>THE CALL (Book Two – Foundational)</u> for a detailed discussion of the healthy ministry cycle of a body.]

Our ministry model (See Resource #4 at the end of this book) is based on partnerships with churches. It is beneficial if a pastor is supportive of building in a community. A pastor, however, that has the vision to commit to, to participate in, and to supervise the work, like Eliashib the high priest, is a blessing from God. That person is a rare gem. And the possibilities that a community will be impacted for the kingdom are greatly increased.

> PRINCIPLE: A pastor who is committed to the work of building is a blessing to the community.

HEALTHY COOPERATIVE MINISTRY

C. How dependent were the workers on one another?

The sections of the wall were built by groups or teams. The people had to work together - different personalities, different skills, and different gifts. But they had the same work. They had to cooperate and they had to tolerate.

My coworker, Hunter, and I took a group from Boyz Club to the beach for a retreat. Well, that statement is not entirely accurate. I took my family to the beach for spring break. We rented a house there. Later in the week, Hunter, being the servant that he is, drove his son and 8 young men from Boyz Club to join us at the house for the retreat. The trip was a reward for Boyz Club members that completed the Boyz Club Foundational Bible Study. We went to the ocean, rode a ferry to the North Carolina aquarium at Fort Fisher, played Putt-Putt and enjoyed other beach activities.

Hunter and I are an interesting team. Hunter is older than I am. He is a single parent raising his son. I am married and the father of 3 children who were young at the time of the retreat.

Hunter is a salesman. Through his charm, he connects with people immediately. Over the years, Hunter has used those connections to obtain resources for Boyz Club. He is always bringing clothes, soccer gear and prizes for the Boyz Club members. I can never keep up with Hunter's many enterprises. He wears so many "hats" that it makes my head "spin" to think about them all. To hear Hunter tell about it, it makes his head "spin" as well. Like many salesmen, linear organization is not his primary talent.

Hunter is also a servant. He is so sensitive to the needs of others. During that beach retreat, I watched in amazement at the way that Hunter served not only 9 young teenagers, but my family as well. Hunter wanted to serve the meals; then he was the first one in the kitchen doing the dishes. He was cook, maid and chief bottlewasher. If any guys wanted to play a game, Hunter facilitated it. Hunter was the first person to respond to any need that arose.

I, on the other hand, am a lawyer. I have worked at the same firm for over 20 years. I am organized and rational. I think progressively and with foresight. My role was to bring some organization and planning to the retreat. I like order. If any young man got out of line, I "sat on them" while Hunter patiently encouraged them.

I can also teach. We had morning and evening devotionals during the retreat that I presented. I must confess that I did not do many dishes. I need to learn from Hunter and to grow in service.

That retreat emphasized what I already realized: Hunter and I are very different people. We simply act differently, think differently, and function differently.

In that type of team dynamic, it is either going to be wonderful or it is going to be awful. It is going to be wonderful when you each respect the strengths the other person brings to the ministry. So you exercise patience with a different approach. Or it is going to be awful when you do not have patience with inherently conflicting personalities and disparate function. So you fight like cats and dogs.

But here is the bottom line: Hunter and I need each other. We are both committed to the ministry the Lord gave us. Through cooperative and deferential attitudes, we were able to conduct a retreat that many years later some of the young men (with whom Hunter and I still have a relationship) talk about.

The businessmen and the ruling officials who built the wall illustrate the variety of gifts necessary for the work of building. Many merchants are consummate salesmen. My friend, Hunter, is a salesman. In his own words, he can "sell ice to an Eskimo along with the freezer to keep it in." Through the years, I have watched in awe as Hunter successfully makes an initial contact – the connection – with a person in the community. This gift is necessary for evangelism and relationship.

The ruling officials were administrative. They represent the gift of facilitation – the ability to keep a ministry functioning through provision of resources and organization of events and participants through planning. This gift is necessary to keep the work functioning.

REJOICING IN DIVERSITY

One of the ironies of God's gifts is that one gift needs another gift that is most unlike it. The person that you need the most often has a personality that you dislike. It is as if the Lord ordained that we learn tolerance and humility in order to obey Him and to overcome.

> PRINCIPLE: The gift that we need is the one most unlike our own.

"But to each one is given the manifestation of the Spirit for the common good." I Cor. 12:7. These gifts are different. But each gift has a God-given function. And each gift must cooperate with other gifts in order to honor the Lord and to do His will. It is classic teamwork used to build a wall.

Forging partnerships between diverse gifts is a key to building effectively. These partnerships develop on a personal level. The workers were highly dependent on one another. Personal relationships in the community in which a disciple is building are a resource. Relationships within a body are a resource as well. Each person has strengths and each person has weaknesses. How are weaknesses covered? By the strengths and talents of others. If I have a relationship with a person, I can receive the benefit from his gifts. I can avail myself of those gifts and talents to the extent that I have relationship. Mutual submission yields resource.

> PRINCIPLE: Multiple gifts operating in submission to one another reflect mature ministry.

Forging partnerships between diverse ministries is a second key to building effectively. The workers of Jerusalem were required to cooperate within the group building their section of the wall. It is blessing when churches, ministries and other organizations unite to impact a community. They form a consortium and function as members of a team who recognize the importance of restoring their section of the wall – their community.

The wall building teams in Jerusalem also had to coordinate with other teams building around them. The sections of the wall needed to meet – to join. Each team had to harmonize their plans with the plans of its adjacent teams. Furthermore, each team relied on their neighbors to help defend the wall and to protect their flank from any outside attack. Today, churches and ministries in one community must cooperate and support churches and ministries working in nearby communities.

Partnerships between ministries; partnerships between churches; partnerships with governments, businesses or other charitable organizations – all of these partnerships can assist the work. These partnerships develop on a corporate level. Effective partnership occurs at the level of leadership. Effective partnership occurs when the leaders of the organizations meet, interact, and develop relationship. Resources, information, and workers are shared to achieve common goals in the community. And the heart of the organization for ministry is shared.

There is a tendency for leaders of churches and ministries to assign surrogates to attend community meetings or unity efforts, and they report back. This delegation reveals that priority is not accorded to the ministry partnership. For the partnership to be effective, the leaders themselves must commit to the partnership and do what leaders do. Leaders lead.

> PRINCIPLE: Forging ministry partnerships is a primary key to building in a community.

MEDITATION: "As for Titus, he is my partner and fellow-worker among you; as for our brethren, they are messengers of the churches, a glory to Christ. Therefore openly before the churches show them the proof of your love and of our reason for boasting about you." II Cor. 8:23-24.

1. Why did Paul give such a glowing description of Titus and the other brethren that he sent to the church at Corinth?

2. Paul was certainly a leader and a spiritual father to many of his coworkers, but he calls Titus his "partner." How does the concept of leadership interplay with the concept of partnership?

3. The word translated "messengers" in the above passage is literally the Greek word "apostles." Why did Paul call Titus and the other brethren "apostles"?

4. How do you feel about the persons that God has placed beside you in God's work?

5. Do you treat your coworkers as "a glory to Christ" and openly show them the proof of your love?

REVIEW:

1. The people that built the wall were diverse in gift, occupation, age and status.
2. Consistent kingdom work reflects the love of God.
3. The days of the part-time Christian are over.
4. A pastor who is committed to the work of building is a blessing to the community.
5. The workers were highly dependent on one another.
6. The gift that we need is the one most unlike our own.
7. Multiple gifts operating in submission to one another reflect mature ministry.
8. Forging ministry partnerships is a primary key to building in a community.
9. Churches and ministries should form team partnerships to build in communities.
10. The leaders of churches and ministries must participate for the partnerships to be effective.

LESSON TEN – ISOLATED

Excitement was in the air. It was so tangible, you could feel it. Not only were hundreds of inner city youth and their families being reached, but partnerships between multiple ministries and churches were evident. It was amazing to watch the whole community being impacted by the body of Christ working together.

The most tangible evidence of this cooperation was in the form of block parties. Some churches united to hold a very successful block party in the community in April. Then in August, three churches combined resources for another party right in the middle of the inner city. The police blocked off a public street. We put basketball goals in the middle of the street and ran basketball games there and soccer games in the grass for the youth.

One church was in charge of food and music. A large group of community members and church members danced together in the street. Another church set up multiple booths with prizes, almost like a fair. A third church bought over $6,000.00 in school supplies and gave them away to poor neighborhood children. The event generated energy and exhilaration.

The feedback was tremendous. Afterwards, one neighborhood parent said "This type of event is exactly what this community needs to come together, and to change."

"So we built the wall and the whole wall was joined together to half its height, for the people had a mind to work." Neh. 4:6.

When a body or a group comes together with a plan from God and commits to the work, it is exciting. Success breeds excitement. This excitement no doubt rippled through the people of Jerusalem as they saw the wall begin to rise. The seemingly impossible task of building now appeared possible – even inevitable – as the wall began to take shape.

But Jerusalem had enemies in its midst. Sanballat the Horonite, Tobiah the Ammonite, and Geshem the Arab were all powerful men who previously had free rei(g)n in the city of Jerusalem. Until now, they had only been scornful of the work of building. They offered cute little quips like "Even what they are building – if a fox should jump on it, he would break their wall down!" Neh. 4:3.

Until now.

RESISTANCE

"Now it came about when Sanballat, Tobiah, the Arabs, the Ammonites, and the Ashdodites heard that the repair of the walls of Jerusalem went on, and that the breaches began to be closed, they were very angry. And all of them conspired together to come and fight against Jerusalem and to cause a disturbance in it." Neh. 4:7-8.

The churches and ministries continued to cooperate through the fall. Another church joined the effort for a large party that Christmas. Hundreds of people from the community came to one of the local churches that had a gym and a field. Basketball, soccer, fun games, food, presents and fellowship were all offered along with a wonderful telling of the Christmas story. It was a magnificent community Christmas party!

But the crowning touch was the donation of 70 new bicycles of all shapes and sizes by one of the church partners. The people were elated! One week later, I stood on a street corner in the neighborhood. It was like a bicycle rodeo. Zoom! One child flew by me on a bike. Zip! Here came a teenager on his ride. Zing! Zooey! Two more bikes whizzed by. I felt like a bicycle air traffic controller.

The ministry had arrived!

Then it happened. The partnership disintegrated. One of the churches experienced an internal split. The pastor of that church resigned and left with his supporters. Another church took sides in the dispute, which put it at odds with the remaining members of the first church. A third church withdrew.

Within three weeks, the cooperation that we had been building for years ended. The partnerships were dead.

We were stunned.

Enemies are scornful when you make plans. They will mock, laugh and ridicule when you set out to do the work. But real resistance normally doesn't arise unless those plans produce results ... unless those plans begin to amount to something.

Now that the wall is built to half its height, the enemies of Nehemiah become very angry. The heathen nations surrounding the small remnant of Jews in Jerusalem begin to conspire to come and fight against them. Kingdom building arouses the enemy to rage.

> PRINCIPLE: Effective ministry awakens resistance.

Every worthwhile ministry faces challenges. Any ministry that brings the kingdom of God to an area experiences stiff resistance. There are three major hindrances – all of which now beset the people of Jerusalem:

1. "The thrill is gone." "Thus in Judah it was said, 'The strength of the burden bearers is failing, yet there is much rubbish; and we ourselves are unable to build the wall.'" Neh. 4:10.

Success can be heady. A new work that takes root generates some buzz. But at some point, the excitement of a new ministry wears off. Exhaustion sets in. The work becomes difficult. It begins to feel like a burden.

Often, people quit at this point. They are tired and no longer inspired. Their work was motivated by what made them feel good, not by what their Lord asked them to do through obedience.

Jesus established a standard for discipleship that cuts to the very core of our being. To follow Jesus, a disciple must "deny himself." Mt. 16:24. How a disciple feels about the ministry to which the Lord has called him should not determine that disciple's obedience.

> PRINCIPLE: When the thrill is gone, the disciple must press on.

2. "Attack from without." "And our enemies said 'They will not know or see until we come

among them, kill them, and put a stop to the work.'" Neh. 4:11.

I went to pick up a young teenager, Victor, for Monday night Bible study. Victor's family fled the civil war in Serbia as refugees. Victor came to Boyz Club and showed a lot of interest in Bible study. But he also was inconsistent. He acted flighty, fidgety, and almost fearful at times.

Victor had just moved into a new house. When I knocked on the door, his father answered it. He had a beer in his hand and offered me one. I declined. Victor's father was proud of their new house and wanted me to see it. We walked through the house as his father enthusiastically showed me each room. He talked a mile a minute. In the kitchen, I noticed cases of beer stacked as tall as I was.

I drove Victor to my house for Bible study. Later that night, I took him back home. Victor's father was in the driveway with a beer in his hand. He waved at me and sidled up to the car. He made two or three attempts to speak to me. But Victor's father was so drunk that he could not even put two words together. I told him "Good night" and left.

As I drove home that night I realized that Victor's erratic behavior was a product of his father's alcoholism and abuse.

We often imagine that kingdom ministry is a feel good, free wheeling, well-paved, happy trails journey. In order to take the kingdom of God to this world though - to the people that really need it, the church has to wade into a morass of ugly, distasteful dysfunction and pain. We are trying to reach people burdened with the oppression of sin - people sometimes bound and spurred by forces of hell that are well entrenched in their territory. Jesus Himself said "It is not those who are healthy who need a physician, but those who are ill. But go and learn what this means, 'I desire compassion, and not sacrifice,' for I did not come to call the righteous, but sinners." Mt. 9:12-13.

In essence, the Christian who is truly devoted to life changing ministry will find himself beset by situations that seem hopeless and desolate - humanly and spiritually. He is under attack from the enemy and from the intrusion of helpless dysfunction.

3. "Attack from within." "And it came about when the Jews who lived near them came and told us ten times, 'They will come up against us from every place where you may turn.'" Neh. 4:12.

The Jews of Jerusalem not only heard threats from their enemies without, but they also were pounded by discouragement and fear from their brethren within. It was reported in Judah TEN TIMES that the situation was hopeless. Despair and hopelessness can come from the inside. People surrounding you who are supposed to be your allies - even well meaning people, convey fear and regularly remind you of your weaknesses and failings. They make statements like: "This community will never change."

Every disciple experienced in ministry has "his ox gored." Often, a coworker or fellow church member displays a dysfunction and absolutely pounds that disciple – sometimes publicly. You are humiliated. You feel like you simply can not work anymore – certainly not with that person around. It makes you want to quit.

ISOLATION

Understand what happened to the Jews. It is a weapon of the enemy that he uses to utmost advantage. Up to now in Nehemiah, we have heard about individual enemies - Sanballat, Tobiah and Geshem. But now a change occurs. Because the wall begins to take shape, nations and peoples conspire against the work..."the Arabs, the Ammonites, and the Ashdodites." Neh. 4:7.The Jews are surrounded on all sides. The Samaritans lie to the north. Sanballat was their governor. The Arabs are to the south. The Ammonites are peoples to the east. The Ashdodites are Philistines - the people to the west. These groups of enemies are now banded together against the wall builders in Jerusalem. Even the Jews' own brethren have joined the tidal wave of voices saying "It can't be done." The builders have become isolated, and are now under attack. They alone must fight this battle.

"Your adversary, the devil, prowls about like a roaring lion, seeking someone to devour." I Pet. 5:8. Have you ever watched nature shows about lions on the plains of Africa? How do they hunt? They prowl stealthily around a herd of prey. The lions try to identify the weak; the injured; the young; or the straggler.

When the lions attack, the whole herd runs. But the lions aren't chasing the herd. The lions are trying to separate a victim from the herd. They know if they can isolate the victim from the herd, they can chase it, pounce on it, and kill it.

The lion uses a strategy of isolation first. And then it kills.

> PRINCIPLE: The enemy threatened the Jews through isolation.

Isolation is a device of the enemy. Satan isolates us so he can attack us and beat on us. Satan wants to cover you with disappointment, discouragement, and ultimately disillusionment with the Lord. Satan uses isolation as a tool for loss of love, loss of hope, and finally, loss of faith. Feeling unloved leads to hopelessness which leads to doubt - doubt about yourself, and doubt about the Lord. Satan's goal is to stymie us, so he tries to orient our focus on our own problems. If he can paralyze us with fear... if he can render us idle with disappointment or depression, then we will not be going out to do what the enemy hates most – working to build the kingdom of God.

> PRINCIPLE: Satan uses isolation as a tool for loss of love, loss of hope, and finally, loss of faith.

HOW TO RESPOND

"[T]hen I stationed men in the lowest parts of the space behind the wall, the exposed places, and I stationed the people in families with their swords, spears and bows. When I saw their fear, I rose and spoke to the nobles, the officials, and the rest of the people: 'Do not be afraid of them; remember the Lord who is great and awesome, and fight for your brothers, your sons, your daughters, your wives, and your houses." Neh. 4:13-14.

You wouldn't think that a man who founded scores of churches, converted thousands of people and mentored dozens of ministers would find himself isolated. A man

who turned the world on its ear, wrote a large part of the New Testament, and is considered by many to be the greatest apostle – he just doesn't get cut off.

Paul ministered widely throughout the world over many years. Yet with short time remaining on this earth, he found himself imprisoned, alone, and under attack. In the final chapter of the book that is commonly acknowledged as the last of Paul's epistles, Paul says this: "At my first defense no one supported me, *but all deserted me*; may it not be counted against them." II Tim. 4:16.

During this time, Paul suffered attack from without and from within. "Demas, having loved this present world, has deserted me and gone to Thessalonica... Alexander the coppersmith did me much harm; the Lord will repay him according to his deeds. Be on guard against him yourself, for he vigorously opposed our teaching." II Tim. 4:10a, 14-15.

Like Nehemiah, Paul had to deal with the spiritual and emotional challenge of isolation and then attack. But both men knew the Lord and reacted with similar responses.

A. "I stationed the people in families."

Many times the key to understanding a verse or passage of scripture is that one statement or word that seems a little unusual or out of place. In this text in Nehemiah, the statement "I stationed the people in families" strikes me as unusual. I understand why Nehemiah stopped the work on the wall at this time and set up a defensive military posture – a posture analogous to spiritual warfare.

But why did Nehemiah station the people in families?

My friends, Michael and Brenda, have a heart for children. They have an amazing discipleship ministry that has operated for many years. The ministry is very private because it employs perhaps the most effective method of discipleship – family. Michael and Brenda take in foster children – children who are abused or neglected...children who do not have a home or responsible parents. Some of the children stay for a few weeks or months. Others stay permanently, and Michael and Brenda adopt them.

At last count, Michael and Brenda had cared for 84 different foster children through the years.

One day, Brenda told me about one of the children they had adopted. He had been abused as a child by his parents. When he came to Michael and Brenda, he struggled with deep emotional issues and problems. He was now a teenager, and his dysfunctional actions seemed to increase. Brenda told me that at times the circumstances seemed almost unbearable.

Here is what Brenda said: "At times, either Michael or I reach the end of our rope. Our son's actions make one of us feel hopeless. Sometimes, I want to give up. But it's strange. At that point, Michael hangs in there and he encourages me to remember that no situation is hopeless if God is present.

"At other times, Michael wants to give up. But then, I am okay. I remind Michael of how much love we have for our son and how much God loves our son. Our love for our son ministers God's love to him. Giving up and abandoning him would mean a failure of that love.

"So far, we have never reached the point where we both want to give up at the same time. I don't know what would happen if we did."

It struck me that Michael and Brenda could keep going for one reason – they had each other. If Michael or Brenda functioned alone, he or she would have given up long ago, and the care for their wards abandoned. But Michael and Brenda sustained each other.

At the crucial time of isolation, surround yourself with the people closest to you. Draw support from the saints that you trust the most. Nehemiah formed the people in families for support. Paul sought help from his friends in his letter to Timothy. "Make every effort to come to me soon...Pick up Mark and bring him with you, for he is useful to me for service." II Tim. 4:9, 11b. Paul knew that he needed help from his closest brethren at this point. He sought to surround himself with support.

> PRINCIPLE: In times of isolation, find support from intimate friends.

The truth is, we all need help. We are afraid of being judged as ungodly if we cry for help. But there is a difference between sanctified and sanctimonious. There is nothing wrong with the words, "Hey, I need help." It may be the difference between standing or falling. We need to cultivate intimate relationships for times of crisis so that we can draw from our support system.

Note that the time to cultivate intimate relationships is **before** the time of crisis. The relationships need to be in place before a time of crisis, because at the time of crisis, it is often too late to develop a relationship of mutual trust, deep communication and intimacy.

B. "But the Lord stood with me, and strengthened me."

"At my first defense no one supported me, but all deserted me; may it not be counted against them. But the Lord stood with me and strengthened me..." II Tim. 4:16-17a.

At this time of deep trial, rely on your Source. Remember Lesson Two of this book when we discussed the foundation for the work:

> "This is the foundation for ministry: Intimacy ... A strong and close relationship ... A deep and abiding Presence ... The hand of the Lord on our life and activity...
>
> "Prayer is the foundation for everything that we do. A disciple connects to the Source through prayer. This life connection is cultivated by time - time spent with the Lord ... time in prayer ... time in meditation ... time in seeking ... time in exaltation."

Now – at this crucial point – the point of exhaustion, the point of attack due to dysfunction or opposition, the point of despair - now is the time that you draw upon the Foundation that you have laid in your life. You draw from the Source Himself.

That is what Paul did. The Lord "strengthened" him. That is what Nehemiah encouraged the people to do: "Do not be afraid of them; remember the Lord who is great and awesome!" Neh. 4:14b.

> PRINCIPLE: At the critical time, draw strength from the Source Himself.

At the time of trial, rejoice in the Lord. We have a good God and that is cause for rejoicing. The circumstances may be dire, and our emotions may be low, but God - our "great and awesome" God - always loves and always stands above. When there is no other reason for joy, He is still our Comfort and our Friend. Choose to rejoice in *Him*. "Then those who sing as well as those who play the flutes shall say 'All my springs are in you.'" Ps. 87:7 (NKJV).

PRINCIPLE: Rejoice in Him at all times, and especially in the rough times.

If the Lord is the Source of your life and ministry, you will survive and overcome the attack. If He is not your Source, you will wilt in the face of resistance.

C. "Fight for your brothers, your sons, your daughters, your wives, and your houses."

Both Nehemiah and Paul had clear and distinct calls from the Lord. Paul knew exactly what God called him to do. "But when He who had set me apart, even from my mother's womb, and called me through His grace, was pleased to reveal His Son in me, that I might preach Him among the Gentiles..." Gal. 1:15-16b. Paul was called as an apostle to the Gentiles. When God calls you to a people, He gives you a love for them.

At the point of despair, Paul remembered his call, and he remembered the people to whom He was called. "At my first defense no one supported me, but all deserted me; may it not be counted against them. But the Lord stood with me and strengthened me, in order that through me the proclamation might be **fully accomplished, and that all the Gentiles might hear...**" II Tim. 4:16-17a. Paul could not forget the Gentiles to whom he was called. They needed to hear! Paul was confident that the Lord would not fail them, but would accomplish the work which He had ordained. So Paul kept going.

Nehemiah knew what God had put in his mind to do for Jerusalem and for its people. Neh. 2:12. At the moment of crisis, he remembered the people to whom he was called, and encouraged his coworkers to remember them as well. "Fight for your brothers, your sons, your daughters, your wives, and your houses!"

In my own life, I have faced discouragement many times. People or events upset me. I wanted to quit. Then I remembered the young men that I worked with. In my mind I saw their faces and thought of their lives - both present and future. I knew that I had to keep working – because of them.

> PRINCIPLE: Remember the people to whom you are called.

So Paul and Nehemiah fought the good fight against their opponents. And as Paul recounts his battle against isolation, he also tells us the result:

"At my first defense no one supported me, but all deserted me; may it not be counted against them. But the Lord stood with me and strengthened me, in order that through me the proclamation might be fully accomplished, and that all the Gentiles might hear; **and I was delivered out of the lion's mouth.**" II Tim. 4:16-17.

> KNOW YOUR SOURCE. KNOW YOUR CALL. KNOW YOUR PLACE ON THE WALL.

MEDITATION: "My flesh and my heart may fail, but God is the strength of my heart and my portion forever." Ps. 73:26.

1. In what ways is God your portion? What does that mean to you?

2. Have you cultivated relationships of intimacy and regular accountability upon which you could rely in times of crisis?

3. Has God placed a call in your life to which you cling in times of crisis?

4. If your church or ministry faced a severe crisis, do you have outside persons or groups that your body could call for assistance?

REVIEW:

1. Effective ministry awakens resistance.
2. When the thrill is gone, the disciple must press on.
3. The Jews were beset with exhaustion, and by attack from without and within.
4. The enemy threatened the Jews through isolation.
5. Satan uses isolation as a tool for loss of love, loss of hope, and finally, loss of faith.
6. In times of isolation and attack, find support from intimate friends.
7. At the critical time, draw strength from the Source Himself.
8. Rejoice in Him at all times, and especially in the rough times.
9. Remember the people to whom you are called.

LESSON ELEVEN – FORMING A BODY

"[T]hen all of us returned to the wall, each one to his work." Neh. 4:15b.

At the beginning of the Revolutionary War, Henry Knox was a bookseller in Boston and Ethan Allen was a farmer in Vermont. Ethan Allen joined a militia group called the Green Mountain Boys with other farmers and settlers. They were not professional soldiers, but they were devoted to a cause based on the idea that "all men were endowed by their Creator with certain inalienable rights." They took action and attacked strategic Fort Ticonderoga located in northern New York. The Green Mountain Boys succeeded in surprising the British garrison there. Ethan Allen demanded surrender by the fort's commander. "By what authority?" the British commander asked. "In the name of the great Jehovah and the Continental Congress!" Allen thundered. The commander surrendered the fort.

Henry Knox' home city, Boston, was occupied by over 8,000 British troops. The people of Boston felt oppressed by the military rule. Knox had read numerous books on military tactics and artillery. He and the other American commanders surveyed the topography of Boston, and conceived a plan to change the city's plight. But the plan required the resource of heavy artillery – heavy artillery that the American army did not have. Knox proposed a daring scheme.

Knox took a contingent of men to Fort Ticonderoga which, thanks to Ethan Allen, was in American hands, and retrieved 60 cannon. With 80 teams of oxen, Knox and his men dragged 60 cannons 300 miles in the snow. It took them 56 days to make the trip back to Boston with the cannons.

When they arrived, by cover of night, the Americans positioned the cannon on Dorchester Heights overlooking Boston and covered the city from strategic positions. On one day the British commander firmly controlled the city. The next morning he woke up and faced a wall of cannon. One day he had power and rule, but the next day there was a greater power above him.

One British captain wrote that the American fortifications "appeared more like

magic than the work of human beings."

Like the citizens of Boston, Nehemiah and the people of Jerusalem found themselves surrounded by the enemy. The work had progressed like gangbusters until the wall was built to half its height. Then the enemy reared its head and the work stopped. But the builders did not retreat. They just protected the gains they had made. Nehemiah retrenched and then he retooled.

STRATEGIC PARTNERSHIPS

The people of Jerusalem wanted to build again. But in order to go forward, they needed to change their approach. Nehemiah put the people back to work on their sections of the wall, but he adjusted the method of the work. Nehemiah made major changes in the building plan.

First, Nehemiah reconfigured the teams of workers, and instituted a new type of ministry partnership.

We were stunned. After the success of the block parties and especially of the large Christmas party, we were flying high. When the church partnerships disintegrated in just a couple of weeks, it was a blow. It was if something or someone had shredded our team.

I studied the situation hard and I prayed. We had been hit hard, and I didn't want it to happen again. What could we do?

I did something that I should have done long before. I knew a number of people that were strong in prayer and intercession. They didn't work "in the field" with us, but the Lord had given them an essential gift.

One by one, I approached the prayer people and asked: "If I send you a regular ministry update and detail our prayer needs, will you commit to pray for us?"

They readily agreed. I began sending frequent outreach prayer requests, and still send them today.

"And it came about from that day on, that half of my servants carried on the work while half of them held the spears, the shields, the bows, and the breastplates; and captains were behind the whole house of Judah." Neh. 4:16.

Under the new strategy, Nehemiah paired the workers on the wall with armed warriors. He combined the offensive ministry with the defensive.

The workers resumed their work at the wall. These workers are the ministers on the front lines doing the work of the Lord to establish an area under His rule and control. The workers represent persons, teams, ministries or even churches. They are the people "on the ground" functioning in close, relational ministry. The workers engage at the point of contact – light going into darkness.

The workers themselves were armed as they worked (Neh. 4:18). Weapons are analogous to spiritual weapons such as prayer, intercession, vision and discernment. Even though the workers were personally armed, they still needed support and protection from experienced warriors.

> PRINCIPLE: The workers are ministers doing the work of the Lord in the field.

To support the workers, armed warriors stood guard. They watched and stood ready to thwart any attack of the enemy. These warriors are analogous to those called to pray and intercede. They provide protection and security for those persons doing the work – a type of spiritual cover. The prayer warriors teamed with workers so the workers could do the work.

> PRINCIPLE: The warriors provide spiritual cover and protection through prayer and intercession.

DIFFERENT GIFTS, BUT THE SAME WORK

The gifts of the worker and of the prayer warrior are very different. Workers are active. They have a dynamic personality. Pragmatic and aggressive, they sally forth courageously to convert, preach and teach. Front line workers are ministers called to the work. They need the resolve of the Lord's call to hold them in the trenches when the fight becomes intense and difficult. Because of their gifts, it is sometimes hard for them to sit still in silence and intercession.

Prayer warriors, on the other hand, are often withdrawn. They minister in the closet. Chances are good that a person who is steeped in prayer has suffered hurt and rejection in his life. At some point, that person turned to the Lord for succor, comfort, and grace. Often, the last thing he is inclined to do is to go work "on the front lines" and experience more rejection.

Many times the worker and warrior personalities clash. A prayer warrior looks out and sees the workers flitting here and there – "Look at those worker bees flit - buzz, buzz, buzz. Where is the honey, dude?" The workers see the prayer warriors sitting there, seemingly doing nothing. They say, "Well, there sit the fruits, nuts and flakes."

But each gift desperately needs the other. They are different gifts, but they engage in the same work. They have different function, but the same goal. By teaming together in this fashion, the work on the wall is able to proceed in the face of bitter opposition. That teamwork is the purpose of my regular "outreach prayer update" which I send out to people of prayer.

> PRINCIPLE: Each gift desperately needs the other.

THE NEW MODEL IN ACTION

Here is a message from one of my close coworkers, Hunter:

Hello, My Good Friends;
I just had a wonderful conversation with David. He has such Energy. He had visited with the Kpa family and delivered food. This is great!
Last Saturday I delivered a donated bike for the Kpa boys to share. Normally, this is greeted with great enthusiasm. There was obviously something wrong. I discovered that they didn't have a place to live. The family/relatives they had been living with had not wanted them there for some time now. That weekend, the dad and one boy stayed with one Montagnard family; the mom and two more sons stayed with another family; and my son

and I took the two younger boys. I have worked with this family for one and a half years - I think I know the boys pretty well. You could see the fear and uncertainty on their faces; and the two younger boys were not handling this well at all. In fact Kuok, who is frequently WILD with energy, was crying.

Ours is a small church and a year and half ago, I doubt many even knew who the Montagnard people were! Well, they know now... I sent out an email explaining their needs to my fellow council members. Within 24 hours we had $1,000 for them. I met with the family Monday morning and helped take care of the little apartment on Lynn Street. These are proud, hardworking people who want to provide a home and education for their children. The family had enough for the security deposit. Their rent is now paid one month in advance, and there are still some funds in reserve for them. Saturday we will deliver a large dining table with six chairs, a sofa, and beds for EVERYONE. These 5 boys have never had beds in their entire life. I imagine they will feel like royalty Saturday night sleeping in their own beds.

Bon unfortunately quit school saying he "couldn't learn any more." Ban (8th grade) has stayed with the tutoring this past summer and all school year. He is absolutely amazing. This past summer he was thrilled to read a five letter word. He has advanced *at least* 6 grade levels in his reading just this year. Unfortunately probably not enough to pass his end of grade exams. But I am meeting with him and Thoan (and others) tonight. If they are on the "border line" there are provisions for them to take an alternate test. (I will file those papers with their schools tomorrow). If we could just start tutoring all of them at a young age...

GOD IS GOOD and He still takes care for His children...

Because of his ministry, my friend, Hunter, had a relationship with the family in poverty. He had connection with the family and discerned their needs. But Hunter sought resource from other ministries. In the report from Hunter, he mentions three different types of assistance – food ministry, tutoring and rent. These resources came from three different churches, but they collaborated through Hunter's work on the ground to help this family. Resource ministries are also a key component to the work.

Here is a model for unified wall building:

A. **GROUND TROOPS** – In the story above, Hunter is a worker on the ground. The "ground troops" are the churches or ministries that take responsibility for the neighborhood or community. They are the persons who do the work on the "front lines." They live in or maintain a constant presence in the community, and bring the kingdom of God to the hearts and lives of the people of the community.

The ground troops are essential to the work! Without their organic and relational work in discipling others, the work is not effective. But the ground troops need help.

B. **CHAIN OF SUPPLY** – The second type of ministry is a "resource ministry." This ministry focuses its efforts on meeting a specific need on a larger scale. The area of need may be food, jobs, education, worship, or housing…the list is endless. In the story above, the three churches acted as resource ministries for Hunter.

A resource ministry can still do work on the ground in an area, but its primary role is to support and assist other ministries working on the ground with a particular resource. The front line workers are the contact point to the communities. They see and discern the real needs. But they require assistance to meet the needs they encounter. The resource ministries provide this layer of support.

C. **COVER OF PRAYER** – Finally, all ministries need prayer support. The prayer warrior provides this cover, and gives direction as the Lord reveals it.

In Nehemiah's adjustments, the warriors stood guard "on site." There they could react immediately to circumstances that arose. On site, intercessors can play a greater role in the ministry. They see what needs prayer immediately. They engage in targeted prayer and focus on specific needs. We encourage ongoing, independent intercession for the ministry, but we also encourage prayer walking and prayer on site at ministry events.

> PRINCIPLE: The work requires front line workers, resource ministries, and prayer cover.

"A REMARKABLE INTERPOSITION OF PROVIDENCE"

The American Continental Congress knew that they needed help from Almighty God in their fight against the most powerful nation on earth. On more than one occasion, the Continental Congress by resolution called for days of prayer, fasting and humiliation before the Lord on behalf of the American cause.

The revolutionary forces of the American army had troops on the ground near Boston. They stood on the front lines ready to fight. But they did not have the fire power to retake Boston. Their plan to free Boston required a resource that they did not have – cannons. Henry Knox supplied this resource through his daring plan to bring cannons from Fort Ticonderoga.

When the British commander in Boston, General Gage woke up and saw the American positions on Dorchester Heights, he immediately planned an assault on the American positions. After all, the British had previously attacked and overwhelmed strong American positions on Bunker Hill and Breed's Hill. The British planned an amphibious assault on Dorchester Heights. Thousands of British troops marched to long boats for embarkation at the next high tide.

But the British never got on the boats. A storm came up suddenly with near hurricane velocity winds. With thick snow blowing sideways into wind-driven waves, an amphibious assault was rendered impossible. The British postponed the assault for days due to the intervening inclement weather. By the time the storm ended, the American positions were so strongly fortified that an assault was out of the question.

The British had to evacuate. On March 17, 1776, General Gage and 8,000 British troops boarded ships in Boston harbor and set sail for Nova Scotia. Without a single casualty, the Americans retook Boston. The authority of the city changed and years of occupation were lifted.

The commanding American general, George Washington, wrote that the storm that

thwarted the British advance represented "a remarkable interposition of Providence."

(Source for stories: <u>The Light and the Glory</u>, by Marshall and Manuel)

Aided by this remarkable interposition of Providence, the Americans combined frontline troops and resource to free Boston. The prayers of the church today prompt the same divine interposition in our lives and ministry on a daily basis.

But the American army needed one more thing to execute their plan. It is the same thing that Nehemiah used to build a wall, and that our ministries need for maximum effectiveness.

MEDITATION: Read II Cor. 9:8-15 (NASB)

1. What is "the harvest of your righteousness" (v. 10)?

2. To what does "the liberality of your contribution to them and to all" refer (v. 13)?

3. How important was prayer for one another to Paul (v. 14)?

4. What can you do to incorporate prayer ministry into the work in your area?

5   What resources are available for the work in your area?

REVIEW:

1. The builders did not retreat. They retrenched.

2. Nehemiah paired the workers on the wall with armed warriors

3. The workers are ministers doing the work of the Lord in the field.

4. The warriors provide spiritual cover and protection through prayer and intercession.

5. The warriors were present "on site."

6. These are different gifts, but they have the same work.

7. Each gift desperately needs the other.

8. The work requires front line workers, resource ministries, and prayer cover.

LESSON TWELVE – FORMING A BODY (PART TWO)

Here is an outreach prayer update sent to my prayer list:

"David, today has been a great day in the kingdom of God!"

This statement from Jack Wolfe of the Urban Eagles still rings in my ears. The statement is remarkable not only for its content, but for the circumstances under which it was spoken.

Jack and his wife, Julia, along with their baby, live in the Beech Apartments on Central Avenue. They serve as urban missionaries to the many people groups there. The night before, a fire had broken out in one of the apartments. It burned a large part of an apartment building. Thankfully, no one was injured. But 13 people were displaced from their homes, and those poor families lost almost every possession that they had.

Jack and Julia were "on site" though, and able to react quickly to help the affected families. The Red Cross came to offer emergency assistance. Jack contacted Dale of Love, Inc. who helped arrange a furniture delivery through Beds for Kids. David of the Commonwealth Food Pantry came from his work and pulled boxes of food supplies. Members of Renewal Church met other needs.

The "great day" that Jack described was the Body of Christ in action. The displaced families needed resources. Jack and Julia had a relationship with resource ministries that were able to provide help.

But the resource ministries needed some one "on the ground." Those ministries were able to assist because Jack and Julia lived and worked at the place of contact. For effective urban ministry, both ministers on the "front lines" and resource ministries to support those front line ministers are essential.

But something else is necessary...people of prayer willing to support, protect and cover through prayer. Both the ministers at the place of need and resource ministries need prayer. Thank you for your willingness to give this support.

Summer is an amazingly busy time for many of our local ministries. Here are some prayer requests…

THE COVER OF AUTHORITY

"…and captains were behind the whole house of Judah." Neh. 4:16

Henry Knox had a plan. The American army camped close to Boston. They were trained and willing to fight. But the plan required a resource that the Americans did not possess – artillery. Ethan Allen and his Green Mountain Boys provided this resource through their capture of Fort Ticonderoga and its cannon.

Execution of the plan, however, required detailed coordination. The task of transporting the cannon to Boston was daunting. After the trip, the plan called for installation of multiple cannon batteries overnight in a way that did not alarm the British.

Execution of the plan could only be achieved through coordinated command.

The three types of ministries – frontline workers, resource ministries, and prayer cover - are analogous to the three major branches of military service. The Army provides ground troops for combat. The Navy is essentially a resource ministry. The Navy insures resource by its protection of shipping and supply, and by its transportation of troops and equipment to strategic locations. The Air Force offers air cover like prayer warriors.

But these ministries, like the branches of the military, require coordination. They need a connection point – a central command to coordinate their efforts and to communicate needs, opportunities, resources, and strategy. Without this coordination, there is confusion and a waste of resources and effort.

Building a wall requires an important attitude: A willingness to coordinate with other ministries and churches. That coordination can occur through a person, a committee, or an organization. Each person and ministry must make a vital commitment: A willingness to submit to spiritual authority.

The Lord has a vision and a plan for your community. He grants to persons and organizations the authority to understand, to communicate and to fulfill His plan. Acknowledgement of, alignment with, and submission to, that authority delegated by God is necessary to build a wall.

Submission to authority is counterintuitive to our human instinct of personal independence and function. Nonetheless submission is necessary to function as a part of His Body. Are you an individual, or are you part of a Body? One of the major themes of scripture is that God intends His followers to function as part of a Body.

> PRINCIPLE: Submission to spiritual authority is necessary to fulfill God's plan.

In the fourth lesson <u>The Appointed Time</u>, we discussed how God granted authority to Nehemiah in the form of call and empowerment to do the work. God gave Nehemiah revelation of His plan, and He granted to Nehemiah authority over the work. But Nehemiah submitted himself to earthly authority. Nehemiah submitted to the king's authority until the king gave him authority to go to Jerusalem and do the work.

Likewise, a disciple working in the kingdom should be subject to proper spiritual authority in his life and work. Even after the disciple is called by God and given authority in his area of work, submission to authority must continue. Authority provides cover for the disciple and for the work. Here is a basic principle:

> PRINCIPLE: A person can not exercise authority unless he himself is subject to it.

The same principle is true for every church, ministry or organization – it must be submitted to spiritual authority established by God.

Every person who has played on a team or has watched many games has seen "that guy." That guy has been blessed with immense talent and possesses moves that are the envy of the league. That guy plays with a sense of ownership and class. He was born to play the game.

Of course, that guy knows it. All plays should go through him. When a teammate

has the ball, that guy is calling for it – on occasions screaming at others if a pass to him is not made or not made quickly enough to suit him. When that guy has the ball, he sometimes does magical things with it. But he is reluctant to pass it back to a teammate.

In that guy's world, the game is mainly about him. The team is secondary. Other team members exist as a platform upon which that guy performs. His talent is on display. The game is his showcase. That guy is a "hot dog."

I have coached a few hot dogs in my day. In the middle of the game, I have a word for the hot dog from the person in authority. "You are a special player. So I have a special place for you. It is a seat here on the bench beside the coach. That way we both can watch a team play."

The city in which I work, Charlotte, North Carolina, must be unique. In Charlotte, every one wants to be the "mother ship." Some ministries and churches, especially large churches, act as an entity unto themselves. They obviously don't feel that they need the rest of the Body of Christ. It is a form of corporate isolation. This attitude is self destructive.

Isolation in the context of the Body of Christ is a myth. In fact, it is a disaster. Isolation is how our enemy, the lion, overcomes his prey. In this case, the isolation is doubly foolish because it is self-imposed. There is a fundamental issue which every church or organization must decide: Which is more important – your organization or the kingdom of God? The choice is vital. One leads to death and the other leads to life. My encouragement is to choose life.

UNITY

"And I said to the nobles, the officials, and the rest of the people, 'The work is great and extensive, and we are separated on the wall far from one another. At whatever place you hear the sound of the trumpet, rally to us there. Our God will fight for us.'" Neh. 4:19-20.

As part of his central coordination, Nehemiah instituted the trumpet. When the trumpet sounded an alarm, it meant to gather ready to fight. The trumpet called all to unite and defend against a concentrated onslaught.

Here is the assembly of the Body. Since every person doing the work was important, every person had the support of the full Body if they came under attack. The people worked in separate groups, but through their unity, any opposition faced the force of the full Body.

> PRINCIPLE: A unified Body supports every building ministry.

Here are reasons why unity is necessary to for the church to fulfill God's will for it:

1. <u>Unity maximizes resources and function</u>.

Our ministries overlap. We overlap in location, in participants, and in timing of ministry events. Through coordination, we maximize our effectiveness in each location and in the lives of its people. In Charlotte, we compile and distribute a monthly outreach calendar that helps avoid event and ministry conflicts, and encourages participation in the events.

We identify resource ministries which enables us to offer assistance and expertise in needed areas in a timely and beneficial way.

2. <u>Unity provides a wall of defense for the Body</u>.

"The enemy comes only to steal, and kill, and destroy; I came that they might have life, and might have it more abundantly." Jn. 10:10. Mutual support is necessary for function. Every ministry and every church, just like every disciple, has times of crisis and need. The enemy and the world are eager to overwhelm and to destroy in those times. Like Nehemiah's plan for the trumpet, the aid of the Body is crucial for survival.

In Charlotte, we try not to take offense at our coworkers, and we try to address and resolve conflicts. Consider this: The disciple that you just cut out of your life due to an offense is the very person that you will need in your next crisis.

3. <u>Unity is necessary for completeness of the Body</u>.

"And He put all things in subjection under His feet, and gave Him as head over all things to the church, which is His body, the fullness of Him who fills all in all." Eph. 1:22-23.

Our goal is His fullness. Personally, we are striving for fullness of His Presence and Character within us, and for completion of His work in us and through us. Corporately, we have the same goal. Fullness of the Body implies that each part is inexplicably intertwined and interdependently connected.

4. UNITY OF THE BODY IS A WITNESS TO THE WORLD.

"I in them, and Thou in me, that they may be perfected in unity, that the world may know that Thou didst send Me, and didst love them, even as Thou didst love Me." Jn. 17:23. The world watches the church to see if the church is any different. Is Jesus real?

The church has relationships. The world has relationships, too. And it has arguments, strife, bitterness and broken relationships. Is the church any different? Does the presence of Christ in our body cause us to act differently? Our witness to the world is not effective until the world can see something different in the church – the Presence of Jesus. Then the world will know that God sent Jesus, and that God loved the church.

We work hard to preserve the unity of the body.

BUT...

Nehemiah's plan for the trumpet sounds great! But what are the implications of this plan of defense?

Unity has a price. Remember that many families in Jerusalem built in front of their own houses. When the trumpet blew, those families had to be willing to leave their own houses - their own area of work and ministry - to fight elsewhere. When the trumpet sounded, they abandoned their own homes and their possessions in order to defend the whole city. Corporate defense meant they left their own house defenseless. If they didn't sacrifice personally, the wall might be breached and the whole city lost. Then, the work would be in vain.

> PRINCIPLE: Unity has a price.

To fight together effectively, some times we have to surrender what is important to us.

Are you a worship person? An outreach person? A person in a position of leadership? Some times you have to give that up - to sacrifice your own fiefdom…to give up your own status - to work as a part of a Body.

The teams building the wall are comprised of ministries and churches. If one falters or is subject to attack, the Body needs to run to its aid. Too many times we tend to disdain or even judge struggling ministries or churches. We maybe even feel that their failure makes us look good if we are still standing when they fall. What we don't realize is that their failure weakens us and exposes our own ministry to attack and even defeat. Are you willing to sacrifice to support another church struggling in its area of work?

Principle: Large impact on an area implies that churches and ministries must support one another.

A BODY

At some point, the people of Jerusalem stopped obsessing with their own selves and their personal circumstances, and they became concerned instead with the work that the Lord had for them. At some point, the people broke their attachments to their own property and possessions, and transferred their affections to the city of Jerusalem, and to its people as a whole. At some point, the people coordinated their talents and efforts such that the sum became greater than its individual parts. The people of Jerusalem became a body.

In Lesson Four of this book, we talked about empowerment from the Lord. I have been praying about the keys to empowerment. Here is one key: Your empowerment will be in proportion to the extent that you work as a body.

PRINCIPLE: Your empowerment will be in proportion to your work as a body.

IMPACT

Understand the impact of unity. What happened to the conspiracy to attack Jerusalem? The attack never came. It never occurred. Did the enemies see armed warriors guarding the work? Is it possible the enemies heard about Nehemiah's new plan of defense? Did the enemies understand that they would meet unified resistance? Did the enemies realize that to attack would be costly and decide it was not worth it?

> PRINCIPLE: The full force of a unified Body is the only way to defeat the enemy.

The willingness of the people in Jerusalem to sacrifice so that they worked as a body enabled them to complete the wall. Building a wall is a corporate effort. Nehemiah started the task by giving groups individual responsibility for each portion of the wall. When the enemy rose in resistance though, he found that the only effective way to fight was to unite so that each area of work was fully supported by the whole body. The work of building the wall was transformed from a collective effort of individuals to a true body endeavor.

Here are keys to Nehemiah's revised plan:

> The people gained the IMPACT of PHYSICAL WORK...
> While experiencing the BENEFIT of SPIRITUAL WARFARE.
>
> The people gained the IMPACT of SMALL GROUPS...
> While experiencing the BENEFIT of a LARGE BODY.

MEDITATION: "[B]ut speaking the truth in love, we are to grow up in all aspects into Him, who is the head, even Christ, from whom the whole body, being fitted and held together by that which every joint supplies, according to the proper working of each individual part, causes the growth of the body for the building up of itself in love." Eph. 4:15-16.

1. "[T]he head, even Christ…causes the growth of the body for the building up of itself in love." How does the head cause this growth?

2. What role do individual parts play in this growth?

3. How are the individual parts fitted and held together?

4. How are you fitted and held together to the whole body?

5. How important is coordination of the resources to this work?

6. What prevents unity of the Body of Christ in your city (or area)?

7. In the context of building, what does this scriptural command mean: "Be subject to one another in the fear of Christ" (Eph. 5:21)?

REVIEW:

1. Front line workers, resource ministries, and prayer cover are analogous to branches of the military.
2. Effective work of the ministries requires coordination.
3. Submission to spiritual authority is necessary to fulfill God's plan
4. A person can not exercise authority unless he himself is subject to it.
5. Unity of Christians is a witness of Christ's love to the world.
6. Unity has a price.
7. A unified Body supports every building ministry.
8. Large impact on an area implies that churches and ministries must support each other.
9. Your empowerment will be in proportion to your work as a body.
10. The full force of a unified Body is the only way to defeat the enemy.

LESSON THIRTEEN– CHANGE

My friend, Patrick, is a wonderful coworker. Patrick built some wealth in a family business, and made a number of shrewd investments. Then Patrick came on board with us at Boyz Club. The Lord gave him a heart for the ministry.

Patrick contributed money and resources to the ministry. He devoted a large mountain house that he owned for the purpose of holding retreats for Boyz Club, Girlz Club and other outreach groups. Patrick purchased a 15 passenger van to transport young people to meetings and events. He donated large sums of money to the ministry, but more importantly, he gave his time as a faithful coworker in the ministry.

Patrick also supported some international missions. He made substantial gifts to a ministry in India run by a small United States mission group. One summer, Patrick went to India to see the work of the mission group. When he returned, he gave a report:

"I have been supporting this mission for a long time. They sent me regular reports of the ministry. Many of the requests for money focused on a great need for facilities. At one point, they built a school. Another time it was a Bible training center, and then a church.

"When I arrived in India, my contact person from the mission met me. Over the next few days, we went from town to town touring the ministry's facilities. In the evening, there was an outreach event in the town we were visiting. I was surprised at what I saw.

"On the first day, we went to the Bible training center for a meeting. I had given money to help build it. The center was large and elegant by Indian standards. But when we went in the front door for the meeting, there were dead leaves in the rooms that had blown in through the windows. Dust covered the floors and furniture. I realized that the center had not been used in a while.

"The ministry conducted an outreach event in the town square that evening. The mission had a truck with sound equipment. The group played music and then preached to the crowd. Attendance was pretty good and a few townspeople milled around the edges as they stopped to check out the event.

"The next day, we went to neighboring city. We did the same thing. The mission took the truck to a public place in the town and held a 'revival.' But as we went from town to town each day, I began to realize something. Each evening, it was the same faces in the crowd. The same people attended each event.

"I am glad I went on that trip, but I am also disappointed. What I discovered is that the ministry had great resources with buildings and equipment, but it didn't have many people to use those buildings. The ministry had facilities, but not many participants."

ORGANIZATIONS AND ORGANISMS

Patrick went to see the ministry that he supported. But he wasn't real pleased with what he discovered. He didn't feel that the ministry had much real impact on the lives of people.

What Patrick described is the difference between organizational ministry and organic ministry. Organizational ministry is ministry based on a defined structure. It focuses on form. It offers programs and events supported by buildings and committees. Organizational ministry fundamentally believes "The system is the solution."

Organic ministry is ministry based on people. It focuses on discipleship that addresses needs and issues that are real in people's lives. Organic ministry begins with a relationship with the Lord; then it reaches out to engage in relationship with people. Organic ministry fundamentally believes "Love the Lord your God with all your heart, mind, soul and strength, and love your neighbor as yourself."

The apostle Paul understood organic ministry. He didn't focus his ministry on buildings or programs. "For we are God's fellow-workers; you are God's field, God's building." I Cor. 3:9. Paul knew that the people were his work.

My coworker, Moses, had been working with us in the outreach ministry for a couple of years. Young, talented and reliable – Moses was very gifted. He helped lead Boyz Club every week, then he coached youth soccer teams composed of refugee teenagers.

Moses wanted to go deeper with discipleship – to select a few willing teenagers and meet with them regularly to teach and disciple them. Moses chose a curriculum and formed a "challenge group" with 5 or 6 participants. He met with them weekly to talk, teach, study

and pray.

A few weeks later I had lunch with Moses. He said, "This challenge group has shown me a lot. At one of our meetings, each guy filled out a survey of spiritual gifts and talents. During that meeting, I realized something. I have been around these guys for a long time. Most of them played on teams that I coached. But as the guys worked on the gifts survey, I realized that I could not tell you the gifts of any young person there. I did not know them that well.

"Meeting in the challenge group has been a great opportunity to dig deeply into each person's world. I am now hearing of issues in their lives and problems in their families and schools that I had no idea even existed."

It is possible to participate in a form or type of ministry, and to have no lasting impact on the lives involved. My friend, Moses, influenced young men at Boyz Club and when he coached them on soccer teams. At the point, however, that Moses ministered in a more personal way (small group or one on one), the relationships became more intimate. His impact increased because he ministered at a deeper level.

Organic ministry cares about disciples in the kingdom, and their hearts. It is time consuming and burdensome. It is also real, because it focuses on people and their lives.

Please note that effective ministry requires both organic ministry and organizational ministry. Order is a necessary component of ministry. We need both substance and structure, just as we need both rules and relationship. Organization, though, should support organic ministry. It can assist ministry, facilitate it, and act as an agent of growth.

> PRINCIPLE: Organization should support organic ministry.

The problem arises when the organization – the form, program, or method – takes precedence over the organic. When a method of ministry leads to success, people begin to believe that the form of ministry is the key to the success. Ministries often lock into a form of ministry until it becomes a habit. Human nature loves habits. Habits give us a sense of security and satisfaction.

Religion based on habit, though, is dangerous. It risks dependence on the habit rather than dependence on the Holy Spirit and on love for God and people. At that point, the ministry has lost its foundation. It will cease to be effective in the lives of people because it does not adjust to their needs. It is analogous to a dynamic in which rules take priority over relationship. We need rules, but without the relationships that underpin those rules, the rules are just legalistic guidelines. As in all legalism, condemnation arises when the rule is violated.

A ministry that is based primarily on organization will eventually wither and die, because it does not have life.

> PRINCIPLE: Religion based on habits is dangerous.

Dependence on the Holy Spirit and on love for God and man is vital, especially when a body is trying to transform a community. Contrast religion based on form and habit with the ministry of the disciples in the Book of Acts. As you read through the Book of Acts, the ministry form adapts in each story according to the circumstance and need. Paul was adept at this change. His approach changed according to each situation and each culture, and according to the instant leading of the Holy Spirit.

CHANGE

One compelling reason that organic ministry must take precedence over organization is the need for change. People change and what those people need changes. A ministry that is locked into a specific form or method refuses to change. At some point, that ministry becomes irrelevant.

I met Jin in 1996 when he was 7 years old. When Jin was 7 years old, my teaching, my ministry programs, and my ministry methods were designed to reach a 7 year old boy.

Now, 14 years later, I still have a relationship with Jin. He is 21 years old. But when Jin comes to visit me, I don't pull out a Veggie Tales movie. The way that I try to interact

with Jin now is a little different than when he was 7 years old.

Over the last 2 years, Jin has been coming to our leadership Bible study. What we discussed during our last study was not necessarily appropriate for a 7 year-old boy. Through the years, I changed my plans and methods to meet Jin's current needs. Organic ministry means that I change to address a person's current needs and issues.

> PRINCIPLE: Organic ministry implies that I change to address current needs and issues.

When I read about Nehemiah and his ministry, I appreciate his willingness to change to meet each situation. Nehemiah understood about the need for change. The Lord initially gave him a clear and specific plan of how to rebuild the walls and gates of Jerusalem. But Nehemiah was not locked into that plan heedlessly, even after it experienced some success. Nehemiah continued to seek revelation from the Lord and direction for the work.

Nehemiah understood that the current situation dictated the form and method of ministry. He changed to address the ongoing needs of the people and the work. When serious threats and danger arose, he even stopped the work on the wall. He encouraged the people in the Lord to combat fear and exhaustion. Then, he placed the people in a defensive formation in families.

Next, Nehemiah changed the system for building. Every person doing the work was armed. He assigned half of the people to build and the other half to guard. He implemented a contingency plan for the whole body using the trumpet in the event of attack.

Nehemiah made one other change that illustrates a key to organic ministry.

PRESENCE

For a number of years, my wife and I have hosted young men in our home for a Bible study on Monday nights. Most of these young men are young adults that formerly were members at Boyz Club. They are older now, and want to grow closer to the Lord.

I say that my wife and I host these young men. I am the one who meets with them for Bible study, but my wife cooks for them and serves them. She is the hostess. She spends

most of Monday planning and preparing a large meal for between 10 and 15 people. My wife is an excellent cook. The group eats together, shares and laughs. Then we do a Bible study.

I joke with my wife that these young men love her more than they love me - that they come to Bible study for her cooking. One reason that humor is funny is that it contains an element of truth.

I tell my wife something else about Monday night Bible study: What the young men see and experience from being in our home is more important than what they learn from the Bible study. These young men have a lot of brokenness in their lives. Most of them do not have fathers at home. For those young men to experience how a loving family interacts and to see how a functional household operates is invaluable to them.

When Jorge comes into our house on Monday nights, he says "Hey coach!" Then he walks past me and says "I've got to go say hello to Mrs. Thurman." He goes into the kitchen and he gives my wife a big hug.

"At that time I also said to the people, 'Let each man with his servant spend the night within Jerusalem so that they may be guard for us by night and a laborer by day.'" Neh. 4:22.

In response to the enemies' challenge, one final change that Nehemiah made to the work was that the people stay "on site" 24 hours a day. This change required sacrifice for a number of the people. Some of them lived in neighboring towns or just outside the city. Now, they could not go home at night after working on the wall all day.

But the work took precedence over the comfort and refuge of their own homes. The work was a priority. Their presence was needed for it.

Presence is a core value of our community work. It is important that we go to the community of our work and enter the lives of the people there. If at all possible, we try to rent an apartment or building in the middle of the community. Our events, meetings and ministry center around that location. Even better still is to live in the community and be incorporated into its culture fully.

> PRINCIPLE: Presence is essential to community building.

I think that my friend, Patrick, is an evangelist. When we think of an evangelist, we think of a person that preaches a dividing line gospel. We envision an intense public speaker that challenges people to decide to accept Jesus in large meetings.

My friend, Patrick, is mild-mannered. He is not even a noted public speaker. But Patrick loves people and he knows how to connect with them. Through the years, Patrick has conducted a wonderful visitation ministry. Patrick makes friends in a community, and then he visits them in their homes regularly. He shares in their lives, and for Patrick, this sharing includes the Lord.

And the people love him for it. They are always inviting Patrick for meals, for weddings, for celebrations, and for events. Whole cultures in our city consider Patrick to be their friend.

Recently, a young man whose family came from a foreign country and whose father is a leader in a different faith was married. In that young man's culture, the uncles of the groom travel to the home of the bride, spend the night, and then "bring" the bride to the place for the wedding. That young man's family asked Patrick to be one of the "uncles" for the groom and to go retrieve the bride.

Patrick practices the impact of presence.

Presence is an important part of organic ministry. Through presence, we learn the needs of people. Through presence, we influence people. Our presence communicates that we care about people. Through presence, we discern the changes that we need to make in our ministry.

> PRINCIPLE: Through presence, we impact the lives of people in the community.

THE PROGRESSION

There is a certain rhythm that occurs in ministry - a certain ebb and flow. There are periods of expansion. These days see increase and growth. The ministry is progressing.

Then, something happens – maybe a challenge or an apparent set back. Maybe you have experienced strong gains, but then need to consolidate and to assimilate new people into the ministry. You take stock and regroup. The ministry becomes a little defensive or even decreases a little.

Then you grow again.

It is analogous to our personal lives. We don't progress on a straight line. Sometimes we grow by leaps and bounds. Other times we slip a little bit...or we just need to rest. Two steps forward; one step back. Or so it seems.

This is a normal pattern for long term, sustainable ministry. But the Lord is always at work.

The changes in organic ministry occur for many reasons. Issues may arise that require a different approach. New people (or a new culture) may arrive. Or there may be a desire to go deeper in the Lord.

This dynamic is part of the rhythm of ministry. Reach out and grow; then break down into discipleship groups. Assimilate, and then connect and assign. Our physical bodies grow by creating new cells, and then placing them in their proper place. So it is with the body of Christ.

Sometimes we believe that God gives us a program for ministry and that we just stick to it. But God many times discloses His will in stages of a progression. The Lord will reveal His plan in His time at the appropriate moment. When you begin ministry to the community, function in the revelation that God has given you. But if you experience some success, don't lock into the methods that God has given you so much that you resist change.

Boyz Club began as an outreach ministry to young teenagers who lived in the inner city. The initial focus of Boyz Club was evangelical. At early Boyz Club meetings, we played a lot of games. There was a short lesson or presentation by a guest speaker, followed by snacks and drinks.

Over the next few years, the members grew older. A number of them made confessions of faith, and some of them were baptized. We looked for ways to help them grow in their faith and character. We began a Bible study for some of the older guys. Games still preceded the meetings, but the games were divided into a younger and older age group. At the meetings, two Bible study groups of older youth went to upstairs rooms at the apartment, while the younger members stayed downstairs for a general meeting.

A few years later still, Boyz Club had members that ranged from ages 10-17. The adult leaders were pleased with the progress of some of the older members. We felt that those older members should have the opportunity to train in ministry and to take on leadership roles. So the format of Boyz Club meetings changed again. The meetings themselves began with worship led by 2 or 3 of the older members. Then we presented a short lesson after which we broke into small groups led by the older Boyz Club members. Each small group read Bible passages related to the lesson, discussed it, and then prayed. The adult leaders ("coaches") sat in the small groups to assist as needed, but the older Boyz Club members led the groups.

Boyz Club is only a small part of our community outreach, and only a few of the many changes through the years were described above. The changes that have occurred, however, are illustrative of changes that can occur in ministry. We adjusted our approach to meet the current spiritual need of our members.

If you have read THE CALL (Book Two – Foundational), you note that the changes at Boyz Club described above track the ministry cycle described in it. God sends his disciples (apostolic) with direction (prophetic) to share the gospel with others (evangelical), to care for others (shepherding), and to prepare others for ministry (teaching). There was some intention in the changes at Boyz Club to try to follow and complete this cycle and to help our members mature in the Lord, but the changes were dictated by the current needs and spiritual growth of the Boyz Club members.

> PRINCIPLE: God may reveal a plan in a progression step by step as a disciple obeys.

MINISTRY DEVELOPMENT

Why does God sometimes choose to reveal His plan step by step instead of all at once? God has the power to make us mature immediately. He could infuse our hearts, minds and spirits with immediate fullness. He also could reveal every detail of our future ministry immediately. Why does God work in a progression?

When I had young children, I hated car seats. Car seats existed for the safety of my children. But they were very uncomfortable. I hated car seats because my children hated them.

We often traveled to visit close family in Alabama. The trip was 500 miles long and took a full day of driving. Almost invariably after departure, when we had been driving 20 minutes and gone 20 miles, one of my young children squirmed in their car seat and asked "How much longer do we have to go? Are we there yet?"

A response based on my adult knowledge and experience would have been "No, dear. We have just started and have only gone 20 miles. We have 480 more miles to travel which is 24 times the distance we have already gone. Our trip will take 24 times longer which means you will be in that car seat all day long."

I never gave that response to my child. Such a response would have been too much of a burden for my child to bear. I normally replied "We will be driving a while longer, but we will stop at the next welcome center. Please be patient, dear."

God cares for us as His children. With patience, He helps us reach maturity - never placing burdens on us that we are unable to handle. If God showed us all that we would go through on our journey, it might overwhelm us. Many times, God only allows us to see the next step, because it is all we can handle.

Years ago, if the Lord had showed me what I am doing now, it would have overwhelmed me. I would not have thought it possible.

The second reason that God works in our lives gradually is so we will trust Him each step of the way. This dynamic creates full dependence on the Him. At every juncture, we have to hear from Him and then humbly obey. A step by step process encourages close dependence on the Holy Spirit to cheer and to guide. He who is faithful in little things, is faithful in much. Lk. 16:10.

> PRINCIPLE: A step by step process encourages close dependence on the Holy Spirit.

We had a good run at Williamsburg. The Williamsburg Apartments were located in the heart of our ministry area. Those apartments were one of the primary placement points for refugees in the city, and they were surrounded by 10-12 multifamily housing complexes for low income residents.

For over 12 years, we rented an apartment at Williamsburg for ministry. We wanted to go where the people were. The apartment was used for English as Second Language classes, after school, youth clubs and a clothes closet. Williamsburg also had some great open areas on which we played soccer, football and other games with the children.

One day, though, we heard that the owners were converting the Williamsburg apartments to condominiums. Our apartment was located on the last row. We watched as the building on the first row was vacated, gutted, and then renovated to sell as condominiums. Slowly, the construction progressed toward us – row by row. Our lease was about to end.

We were concerned. Many of our ministry families and children left. They were evicted to accommodate the condominium project. What would happen when we lost our apartment? Would we be able to transition elsewhere? Would the ministry suffer, or would it even end?

The day came when we received the notice. Our lease was being terminated. What happens when your lease runs out?

We scouted the area, and located an apartment in a nearby complex to rent. That complex had an open grassy area, but the owners told us we were forbidden to use it for soccer or other games. Our ministry experienced change and transition.

But the bottom line is that almost all of our families and participants transitioned with us to the new apartment. We learned an important lesson: Programs, events and even locations come to an end. But relationships endure.

> PRINCIPLE: Programs come to an end. Relationships last a lifetime...and then some.

MEDITATION: "Martha, Martha, you are worried and bothered about so many things, but only a few things are necessary, really only one, for Mary has chosen the good part, which shall not be taken away from her." Lk. 10:41b -42.

1. What was Martha doing?

2. The things that Martha was doing, were they helpful and beneficial?

3. What was Mary doing that was so necessary?

4. What was Jesus doing at that time?

5. Were Jesus' actions necessary as well?

REVIEW:
1. Organizational ministry fundamentally believes "The system is the solution."
2. Organic ministry fundamentally believes "Love the Lord your God with all your heart, mind, soul and strength, and love your neighbor as yourself."
3. Effective ministry requires both organic ministry and organizational ministry.
4. Organization should support organic ministry.
5. Organic ministry implies that I change to address current needs and issues.
6. Through presence, we impact a community and the lives of its people.
7. God may reveal a plan in a progression step by step as a disciple obeys.
8. A step by step process encourages close dependence on the Holy Spirit.
9. Programs come to an end. Relationships last a lifetime...and then some.

LESSON FOURTEEN – STRUCTURAL INTEGRITY

Saladin's story is a sad one. Saladin is a dark-skinned 13 year-old boy. Saladin's family is Somali Bantu. The Bantu are a tribe in Africa brought to Somalia as slaves for menial labor jobs. Somalis disdain the Bantu as a lower class. The Bantu were mistreated. During the long tribal civil war in Somalia, many Bantu were killed. Saladin's family fled Somalia and lived in a refugee camp for a few years before they came to America.

After Saladin's family arrived in America, Saladin's mother died. Pursuant to tribal and religious custom, Saladin's father had another wife. When Saladin's mother died, Saladin's father decided to go live with his other wife and their children in another state. But Saladin's father did not want to integrate Saladin and his younger brother into his other family, so he left them. Saladin went to live with his cousin's family.

Saladin's cousin is very poor. Patrick visits that family regularly. They live in a small house in a bad part of town. On one visit, Patrick counted 19 people living in that home in squalid conditions. But the young men in that family come to Boyz Club, so Saladin began attending Boyz Club with them.

Saladin has another problem. Saladin is a special needs child. He is developmentally disabled and is hard to understand. Saladin can't focus for any extended period of time. He moves constantly - wiggling in his seat, waving his arms and talking to himself.

Those of us who know Saladin's story try to show him love and mercy. We want him to experience compassion, acceptance, support and maybe even a little joy at Boyz Club. But not all the other Boyz Club members see it that way.

Last week at Boyz Club, Saladin sat beside another 13 year old boy from a different nation and race. The other boy began to mock Saladin and aggravate him. Saladin said "Stop!"

The other boy continued his mockery.

"Stop it!" Saladin said again. He was defenseless to the ridicule.

The other boy looked at Saladin, leaned over, and whispered "Hey monkey!"

"Hey MONKEY!" When I heard "monkey," I snapped. I controlled my reaction, but something within me snapped.

I was very angry. I immediately took steps to address that slur.

"Then I was very angry when I had heard their outcry and these words." Neh. 5:6.

So far in the Book of Nehemiah, Nehemiah has faced huge obstacles. The challenge to build a wall with limited resources was daunting. His opponents taunted him. They mocked and ridiculed him. Then the enemies of Jerusalem bullied, intimidated and threatened him. They plotted to destroy him.

But through these trials, we do not read that Nehemiah became angry – not until now.

What made Nehemiah so angry?

THE HEART OF THE LORD

There is a "great outcry" in Jerusalem. Neh. 5:1. The poor workers in Jerusalem are under distress economically and socially. Some families are hungry because they can't buy food (Neh. 5:2); some have lost their property because of mortgages or taxes (Neh. 5:3-4); and some have been forced to sell their sons and daughters into slavery because they have borrowed money and can not repay it (Neh. 5:5). This distress is one reason for Nehemiah's anger. He has concern for the condition of the builders.

> PRINCIPLE: Poverty is oppression. Debt is bondage.

Nehemiah had the heart of God toward the poor and oppressed. Here is what scripture says about the poor and needy:

A. Scripture is clear that the heart of the Lord is close to the poor.
Deut. 10:18 – "[God] executes justice for the orphan and the widow, and shows His love for the alien by giving him food and clothing."
Ps. 69:33 – "The Lord hears the needy, And does not despise His who are prisoners."
Isa. 41:17 – "The afflicted and needy are seeking water, but there is none; and their tongue is

parched with thirst; I, the Lord, will answer them Myself, as the God of Israel I will not forsake them."

B. What about the heart of a righteous person like Nehemiah? Does he have the heart of God in this matter? The righteous man has touched the heart of God in this matter. The righteous man is concerned with the needs of the poor - the widow, the orphan, the refugee.
Prov. 29:7 – "The righteous is concerned for the rights of the poor; the wicked does not understand such concern."
Prov. 14:31 – "He who oppresses the poor reproaches His Maker, but he that is gracious to the needy honors Him."

C. Because the heart of God yearns for the poor, God blesses the disciple that ministers to the poor.
Ps. 41:1- "How blessed is he who considers the helpless; the Lord will deliver him in a day of trouble."
Prov. 14:21 – "Happy is he who is gracious to the poor."
Pro. 28:27 – "He who gives to the poor will never want, But he who shuts his eyes will have many curses."
What about the person that neglects the poor? Pro. 21:13 – "He who shuts his ear to the cry of the poor will also cry himself and not be answered."

D. Why is the heart of the Lord so close to the poor? The Lord Himself identifies with the poor, the needy and the oppressed.

Timothy Keller, who is a great resource for such teachings on the poor, says the Lord identifies with the poor because He was poor on this earth. Mt. 8:19-20 – "And a certain scribe came and said to Him, 'Teacher, I will follow You wherever you go.' And Jesus said to him, 'The foxes have holes, and the birds of the air have nests; but the Son of Man has nowhere to lay His head.'"

Jesus became poor for us. II Cor. 8:9 – "For you know the grace of our Lord Jesus Christ, that though He was rich, yet for your sake He became poor, that you through His poverty might become rich." (Source Material: Sermons by Timothy Keller)

E. In fact, the Lord identifies so closely with the poor that taking care of the poor is ministering to the Lord Himself.

Prov. 19:17 – "He who is gracious to a poor man lends to the Lord, and He will repay him for his good deed."

Jesus explained it clearly in Mt. 25:37-40 – "Then the righteous will answer Him, saying 'Lord, when did we see You hungry, and feed You, or thirsty and give You drink?' ... Truly I say to you, to the extent that you did it to one of these brothers of Mine, even the least of them, you did it to Me."

The principle that giving to the poor is giving to the Lord Himself is illustrated in the practice of the tithe. Lev. 27:30 – "The tithe of the land ... is the Lord's; it is holy to the Lord." The tithe is holy to the Lord. It belongs to God.

But in the institution of the tithe in Deuteronomy, something unusual happened every third year (in the seven year cycle). Deut. 14:22-29; 26:1-19. For two years, tithes were dedicated to the Levites and for feasts in the Lord's presence. Deut. 26:11. But in the third year, tithes went to a different place. Every third year, a tithe went to "the Levite, to the stranger, to the orphan and to the widow, that they may eat in your towns, and be satisfied." Deut. 26:12b. That tithe was not given to the priest or for feasting, but to the poor in *the giver's own town*. This charity to the needy of the community is a basic principle of the tithe and its intended use. When it was given to the poor, it was given to the Lord.

EXTREME ANGER

Nehemiah is disturbed when poor wall builders complain of losing their homes, their fields and their families. Neh. 5:6. He is upset because their distress is a threat to the work which the Lord has ordained. Because of poverty, hunger, and oppression, the poor of Jerusalem are unable to work on the wall. But the work has been threatened before.

What incensed Nehemiah greatly was the source of the oppression. The oppression of the poor came not from outsiders, but from their own brethren in Jerusalem! The wealthy in

Jerusalem were enslaving their poor brethren, and seizing their homes, fields and vineyards. "You are exacting usury, each from his brother! Therefore I held a great assembly against them." Neh. 5:7b.

What outraged Nehemiah was that the wealthy in Jerusalem were doing what Nehemiah expected from their enemies! Their treasure was being used for their selfish gain and pleasure, not for God's purposes - to do God's work by rebuilding the wall.

> PRINCIPLE: Nehemiah is angry that the wealthy Jews were acting like enemies of the workers.

STRUCTURAL INTEGRITY

At soccer this past Sunday, I experienced something that brought me great pleasure. There weren't any dramatic events or dynamic sharing. There wasn't even a large crowd.

As young teenagers, the participants on Sunday lived and breathed the game of soccer. A number of them dreamed of being professional soccer players. Now, however, they are older – in their early 20's. They are focused on jobs, school and family. Soccer is now something that they enjoy, but it is secondary. As much as anything, soccer on Sundays is a chance to gather, converse, laugh, hug and "rub shoulders." We play awhile, but then we take a break for water and sit around chatting. They even let me, a man past middle age, play.

Here is what pleased me about that Sunday: The diversity of the participants, and the comraderie of the participants. There was Abu from Somalia; Victor from Serbia; Jin from Vietnam; Kennedy from Congo; Eldin from Bosnia; and Jorge from Liberia. Others came but didn't even play. They just hung out.

As I sat there, I thought back many years. These guys all had been to Sunday soccer as refugee youth. The differences in culture, language and race were larger then. Many of them got into fights. As young teens, they came to Boyz Club and interacted through the activities there. Bridging cultural, social and racial divides was a value we tried to convey. Then in high school, every one of them played on soccer teams that I coached. One of those

years, I had players on the team from nine different countries.

So I sat there on Sunday and soaked it in. These guys weren't just soccer players. They were friends.

And as I sat there, I thought to myself: "This is a picture of the kingdom of God - every tribe, tongue, people and nation." Rev. 5:9.

Nehemiah was working to restore the area of Jerusalem. But Nehemiah knew that restoration of the people could not occur as long as economic oppression of the poor and class discrimination by the "nobles and rulers" (Neh. 5:7) existed. These offenses undermined the very structure of the society from within. They were like huge rips in the fabric that bound the people together as a body.

> PRINCIPLE: A vital element of restoration of the community is the repair of its social and economic fabric.

Nehemiah acted quickly to mend these tears. He called for immediate restoration of the people and their property. "Please give back to them this very day their fields, their vineyards, their olive groves, and their houses, also the hundredth part of the money and of the grain, the new wine, and the oil that you are exacting from them." Neh. 5:11. Nehemiah required the nobles and rulers to take an oath before the priests to honor their promise. Neh. 5:12.

Structural integrity is vital to the work of God among a people and a community. There was another occasion when work of the Lord was changing a city as in Nehemiah, but social and economic inequity dogged a fledgling work. Discipleship and explosive growth was happening, but the integrity of the body was threatened by neglect of a poor underclass.

In the infancy of the church in the Book of Acts, mass conversions occurred in Jerusalem and the believers were "of one heart and soul." Acts 4:32. But in Acts 6, "a complaint arose on the part of the Hellenistic Jews against the native Hebrews, because their widows were being overlooked in the daily serving of food." Acts 6:1.

The fabric of the body was torn. The integrity of the church was threatened by economic inequity – the neglect of widows; and by social inequity – a preference of native Hebrews to the exclusion of Hellenistic Jews (who were Greek).

Like Nehemiah, the twelve disciples acted quickly to bring restoration and reconciliation to the situation. Like Nehemiah, they understood that restoration of the fabric within the body was essential. The disciples knew the impact that attention to the poor would have on the gospel, just as they realized the negative impact on the gospel of discrimination and ignoring the poor. The disciples appointed deacons and assigned to them the task of fair distribution.

> PRINCIPLE: The church can not assert spiritual authority when it discriminates by class or race.

What was the result of restoration of the whole body in the Book of Acts? "And the word of God kept on spreading; and the number of disciples continued to increase greatly in Jerusalem, and a great many of the priests were becoming obedient to the faith." Acts 6:7. The church was strengthened. When the church acts like the body of Christ and cares for the poor and neglected, it is a witness to the world of the tangible impact of the gospel. The word was spreading; the number of disciples increased; and many priests came to faith. Priests were numbered among the poor in Israel. Maybe when the priests saw that the early church took care of the poor, then they were moved to come to the faith.

Do you recall the one thing that the apostles told Paul and Barnabas to do while preaching the gospel? They commissioned Paul and Barnabas to take the gospel to the Gentiles with one important instruction. Did they tell them to be sure and teach the Ten Commandments? No. Did they tell them to be worship in a certain way? No. What one important instruction did the apostles give?

Gal. 2:10 – "They only asked us to remember the poor - the very thing I also was eager to do." The apostles and Paul and Barnabas understood how important it was to take care of the poor - how ministry to the needy went hand in hand with the presentation of the gospel. When you have sowed seeds of compassion, then you have the standing to say, "Let me share with you the gospel."

The care of poor by the body is vital to the work of the Lord. Read scripture, and understand that the gospel and ministry to the poor and oppressed are intertwined.

> PRINCIPLE: Economic restoration and social inclusion are vital to the witness of the gospel.

RESTORATION

This past Wednesday, I went to work as I do almost every weekday. I left work early to pick up food for a poor refugee family. Then I went to Boyz Club for two and one-half hours. It was late when I left Boyz Club.

Then I stopped by the apartment of the poor family to drop off the food. Our food bank program is designed to be relational. Instead of randomly distributing food to strangers, we have sponsors for each family in the program. The sponsors agree to visit the families regularly, to discern the level of need, and to monitor the family's needs. I was the sponsor for this family, but to be honest, I was hoping for a quick exit. It was late, I was tired, and I wanted to get home to eat supper.

But as I entered the apartment with the food, the father of the family motioned me to a small table. In his broken English, he showed me booklets full of forms from the public school system. He didn't understand the forms and needed assistance with them. I sat down and went through two booklets full of forms with him and his family, reviewing and completing each form ...then two more booklets for the next child...and two more booklets for the next child. It took quite a bit of time.

It was inconvenient for me. I came to deliver food. But the family had a different need.

Charity is a strange word. It can mean many different things. There is a type of charity that is very beneficial to the recipient. But there are other types of "charity" that aren't beneficial to the recipient and, in fact, may even be harmful. The challenge of the person practicing charity is to use strategies and methods that are actually beneficial to the recipient.

> PRINCIPLE: Restoration implies charity that is beneficial to the recipient.

One key to beneficial charity is relationship. If you have a relationship with the recipient, you are able to discern their real needs, and to assess the impact of the charity. I intended to deliver food to a family. But their need was assistance in completing school forms. Because I took time to visit and to know them, I was able to meet a real need.

I have always been fascinated by one of the key verses on ministry to the poor. "This is pure and undefiled religion in the sight of our God and Father, to visit orphans and widows in their distress, and to keep oneself unstained by the world." James 1:27. Shouldn't that verse read "to donate money to orphans and widows"? But it doesn't. It says to visit them...to have relationship. When you visit them, you can both show love and provide care.

Also, when you are unstained by the world and its values of selfish accumulation of wealth and personal pleasure seeking, then you give your time and resources to the poor.

> PRINCIPLE: Relationship enhances charitable impact.

"Charity" is a strange word as it relates to our attitude. What is our motivation for our charity?

At Christmas, we have asked church members to buy and wrap gifts for our young members of Boyz Club, Girlz Club and Good Shepherd Club. Some of the presents have been wonderful. But other presents have been old toys that were broken or used clothing that was threadbare and worn at the knees or elbows. What did that communicate to the children when they opened a present like that? It communicated the same thing that the nobles and rulers of Jerusalem conveyed to the poor in Jerusalem. "You are not important to me, and actually nothing more to me than a substandard slave."

If charity is borne out of a sense of obligation, that will be apparent to the recipients. You will do just enough to satisfy your obligation and "throw a bone" to the recipients. They will understand that they are an object of your compulsion.

But if love is the motivation for charity, that love will be expressed through relationship and sacrifice. The recipient will understand that you have Godly love and compassion which is demonstrated to them in many ways.

> PRINCIPLE: Love is the only true motivation for charity.

"And all the assembly said, 'Amen!' And they praised the Lord. Then the people did according to this promise." Neh. 5:13b.

MEDITATION: "And those from among you will rebuild the ancient ruins; You will raise up the age-old foundations; And you will be called the repairer of the breach, The restorer of the streets in which to dwell." Isa. 58:12.

1. Read Isa. 58:1-12. Who are the rebuilders, repairers and restorers in this verse?

2. Why are their actions called a "fast" which God Himself chose (verse 6)?

3. How can you implant in yourself the heart of God in this matter?

4. What actions will this heart prompt?

REVIEW:

1. Poverty is oppression. Debt is bondage.
2. Scripture is clear that the heart of the Lord is close to the poor.
3. The righteous person is concerned with the needs of the poor - the widow, the orphan, the refugee.
4. God blesses the person who ministers to the poor.
5. The Lord identifies with the poor because He was poor on this earth.
6. Taking care of the poor is ministering to the Lord Himself.
7. Nehemiah is angry that the wealthy Jews were acting like enemies of the workers.
8. A vital element of restoration of the community is the repair of its social and economic fabric.
9. The church can not assert spiritual authority when it discriminates by class or race.
10. Economic restoration and social inclusion are vital to the witness of the gospel.
11. Restoration implies charity that is beneficial to the recipient.
12. Relationship enhances charitable impact.
13. Love is the only true motivation for charity.

LESSON FIFTEEN – "REMEMBER ME, O MY GOD"

"Remember me, O my God, for good, according to all that I have done for this people." Neh. 5:19

Barnabas is a wonderful coworker. Sometimes a leader with charisma attends a ministry event. He has a glowing personality, and his bearing shouts "Follow me, people!" That leader acts, talks and walks in a way that causes young people to flock to him. Soon, crowds gather around that leader. But Barnabas is not that type of leader. He doesn't display "flash" or stand out in a crowd.

To the contrary, at a large ministry event Barnabas is likely to be working "behind the scenes." Barnabas is a server. If there is a task that needs doing, Barnabas does it. If there is a role that is essential to run the event, Barnabas fills that role. Barnabas rarely speaks at large events. Yet on Sundays he met with a group of refugees from an Asian country and led them in a Bible study. We are hopeful of cultivating leadership from the group for an ethnic church.

Barnabas is an encourager. One of the first times that I met Barnabas, he asked me "Are you encouraged?" I thought "What an odd question!" But Barnabas is serious. He desires that the saints be edified. If you see Barnabas at a ministry event, he later sends you an e-mail that describes a spiritual gift he saw you exercise. If Barnabas visits your home, he sends a "thank you" card expressing his appreciation for your hospitality. Encouragement is important to Barnabas. That is why I call him Barnabas – the "son of encouragement."

Barnabas is faithful – in big and small things. If Barnabas commits to attend a meeting, he will be there. Barnabas ministered to a needy family that he met. He helped them move to a better place to live. He assisted the young men in their studies. Barnabas is consistent and steady.

Barnabas is rarely the man "up top." He doesn't strive to be the man "out front." But as I have watched Barnabas operate in the gifts and wisdom that the Lord has given him, I have decided this: Barnabas is a leader, and probably a leader of the best type.

Neh. 5:14-19 is an important passage. It is important because in it, Nehemiah describes his method of leadership. Nehemiah was an extraordinary leader - extraordinary in his understanding of authority and in his obedience to God. His method of leadership is instructive.

Nehemiah was governor in the land of Judah. Neh. 5:14. This position was powerful and potentially very profitable. A governor normally used his position to build his personal wealth and prestige. But Nehemiah focused on doing the Lord's work instead, not pleasing himself. Here are Nehemiah's keys to leadership:

A. <u>Attitude of Ministry.</u> Unlike the rulers before him, Nehemiah did not lord his authority over the people. "But the former governors who were before me laid burdens on the people and took from them bread and wine besides forty shekels of silver; even their servants domineered the people. But I did not do so because of the fear of God." Neh. 5:15. Nehemiah saw himself as the servant of God rather than a Lord over other people. Because he feared the Lord, he did not dominate the people. "…and be subject to one another in the fear of Christ." Eph. 5:21.

B. <u>Purpose of Ministry.</u> Nehemiah did not take from the people to benefit himself. "[F]or twelve years, neither I nor my kinsmen have eaten the governor's food allowance." Neh. 5:14. Instead, he used his position of authority to serve his own people and the people around Jerusalem. "Moreover, there were at my table one hundred and fifty Jews and officials, besides those who came from the nations that were around us." Neh. 5:17. Instead of using his power for his selfish gain, Nehemiah used it to benefit the people subject to his governorship.

C. <u>Work of Ministry.</u> Nehemiah participated in the work of ministry himself. "I also applied myself to the work on this wall; we did not buy any land, and all my servants were gathered there for the work." Neh. 5:16. Instead of directing the people to do the labor for him, Nehemiah and his servants shared in the burden of the work.

<u>COUNTERCULTURE</u>

Nehemiah's statement of his leadership stands in stark contrast to the warning that God gave Israel about a king. Here is God's description of the impact of a king in I Samuel 8:

1. A king dominates the people. "This is the procedure of the king who will reign over you: he will take your sons and place them for himself in his chariots and among his horsemen and they will run before his chariots...you yourselves will become his servants." I Sam. 8:11, 17.

2. The king bleeds his people. He takes daughters, young men, fields, vineyards, olive groves, male and female servants, donkeys and flocks. I Sam. 8:13-17. The king takes from the people and does not give to them.

3. The king makes others do his work. "He will appoint for himself commanders...some to do his plowing and to reap his harvest and to make his weapons of war and equipment for his chariots." I Sam. 8:12.

Despite God's warning, the people still desired a king. They wanted a king to fight their battles and to judge them. But most telling is they wanted a king to "be like all the nations." I Sam. 8:19-20. The people wanted worldly leadership like the rest of the nations. They rejected God as their king. "And the Lord said to Samuel, 'Listen to the voice of the people in regard to all that they say to you, for they have not rejected you, they have rejected Me from being king over them." I Sam. 8:7.

> PRINCIPLE: Dominating leadership is worldly leadership.

It is amazing that the Godly leadership offered by Nehemiah is the exact opposite of the worldly leadership offered by a king. Nehemiah's leadership differed from the governors before him. His leadership also differed from the leadership that the world reveres. People today still want a king to "take care" of them. Nehemiah truly acted in a counterculture way.

But that counterculture leadership was necessary. For Nehemiah was trying to restore God as king among the people in Jerusalem, not himself. He was reversing Israel's rejection of God as King, and counteracting the devastation that resulted from that rejection. Let's look at Nehemiah's keys to leadership in more detail.

A. ATTITUDE OF MINISTRY

An effective leader maintains right discernment of his attitude in two key areas: (1) Internal - His opinion of himself (or herself); and (2) External - His view of himself (or herself) in relationship to others.

1. <u>Internal - Himself</u>

Some leaders have a hefty opinion of themselves. These leaders are often gifted speakers blessed with huge promise which "justifies" their large self-promotion. Edgy and eloquent, their bearing shouts "I am the one!"

The apostle Paul admonished every person about this attitude. He said: "For through the grace given to me I say to every man among you not to think more highly of himself than he ought to think; but to think so as to have sound judgment, as God has allotted to each a measure of faith." Rom. 12:3.

When I started practicing law, I had a great mentor. He had talent, but he was also a man from the country with humility and common sense.

One day, after we attended a deposition with other lawyers, he pointed out one of the lawyers to me. "David," he said, "did you see Mr. Crews in action?"

"Yes, sir" I replied.

"He's not very flashy, is he?"

"No, sir" I said.

"David, Mr. Crews is a very nice person. He is meek and mild-mannered. But let me tell you something, he is a very good lawyer. And an effective one, too. Do you know why?"

"No, sir."

"He's a good lawyer because he practices law in accordance with who he is. He understands himself and that enables him to practice law accordingly."

My mentor continued. "You see, David, too many lawyers think that they have to be aggressive world-beaters in order to be effective. But it doesn't work for them because that isn't who they are. The key to effective representation is not so much a certain style. The

key to effective advocacy is this: **Understand who you are and practice law in accordance with who you are. If you are a kind and sensitive person, practice law that way. If you are a mean and ornery jerk, practice law that way. Understand who you are and be who you are."**

Not to think more highly of himself than he ought to think! Understand who you are! Talent is not necessarily a good measure of an effective leader. There are very talented persons who are bad leaders because they have an inflated view of their large talent and ability. They believe their own hype. Effectiveness of a leader is determined not so much by his talent as by his proper understanding of his strengths and his weaknesses. This is "sound judgment."

The impact of healthy self-perception will cause a leader to work in the context of a team. If the leader's esteem is inflated, he thinks he has the "package" and that he can carry the day by his own presence. But a leader who understands his limitations will seek help from others who can join their talents with his talents to make an effective whole. That leader will not be threatened by strong gifts in others, but will seek their assistance to further the work of the Lord in ministry.

> PRINCIPLE: An effective minister understands his own gifts AND his own limitations.

2. <u>External - Others</u>

When I coached soccer, we had some overwhelming wins, and we had some disastrous losses. We whipped some teams, but we also were beaten by some obviously superior sides.

One day we beat a team by a score of 13-0. It was complete domination. After the game, I addressed the team. "Guys," I said "you played okay today. But let me tell you something, I would rather play a team that beat us 6-0 than play a team that we beat 13-0."

-"What?!?"

-"Are you kidding?"

-"No way, coach! I would much rather win!"

"Let me explain," I said. "When you beat a team easily like today, you don't learn very much about yourself. It isn't a challenge.

"But" I continued "when you are beaten by a superior team, it shows you something about yourself in relationship to that team. That loss shows you who you really are. Your weaknesses are exposed and the other team demonstrates to you how to play. A big loss is a catalyst for growth because you understand that you are not the top dog."

The second key attitude of a leader is his attitude toward others. If the leader occupies a position of authority, the attitude of the leader toward those persons subject to that authority is particularly telling.

When you talk with a leader, you can quickly discern where he is coming from. Some leaders approach you from a position of superiority. In their mind, while they are talking to you, they are above you. Their bearing and speech communicate their presumed superiority.

Other leaders approach you from a position of servanthood. They are not above you, but in fact live to serve you.

The apostle Paul also admonished every person about this attitude. He said: "Do nothing from selfishness or empty conceit, but with humility of mind let each of you regard one another as more important than himself; do not merely look out for your own personal interests, but also for the interests of others." Phil. 2:3-4.

Not to think more highly of himself than he ought to think! Let each of you regard one another as more important than himself! This is the attitude of an effective leader.

And Nehemiah tells us the reason for this attitude. "But the former governors who were before me laid burdens on the people...but I did not do so because of the fear of God." Neh. 5:15. Nehemiah's desire was to serve God and Him alone, not to exalt or to glorify himself in any way. Nehemiah feared God. His only interest was God's glory. If any glory came to Nehemiah, he was robbing God of something that belonged to God – and Him alone.

As a leader, do you have any desire to please yourself or to glorify yourself?

> PRINCIPLE: Authority glorifies God alone, not itself.

B. PURPOSE OF MINISTRY

Nehemiah was governor in the land of Judah. Governorship had some perks. It was a position of power and prestige. A governor could use his position to make himself wealthy, fat and powerful. The prior governors had done this. "But the former governors who were before me laid burdens on the people and took from them bread and wine besides forty shekels of silver; even their servants domineered the people." Neh. 5:15b.

But Nehemiah did not take advantage of the authority that God gave him. Over twelve years of rule, he did not eat the governor's food allowance. Neh. 5:14. He did not take money from the people. Neh. 5:15. He did not acquire any land to become a land baron. Neh. 5:16. Instead, Nehemiah fed and served 150 people at his table each day. Neh. 5:17-18.

Nehemiah knew that God gave him authority for a purpose: To serve God's people. If God has given you authority, it should be used to serve Him and to serve people in that area of authority.

> PRINCIPLE: The purpose of ministry is to serve people.

Over 20 years ago, I was the chairman of the Men's Retreat committee at my church. Chase was a gifted teacher and he served on that committee with me. Our job was to plan, organize and run the annual Men's Retreat.

At the retreat, we had teachings on Friday night and Saturday morning. Saturday afternoon was set aside for recreation and reflection. After lunch on Saturday, the committee met briefly. The teachings had gone well. I was getting ready to go play golf with some golfing buddies.

"Chase," I asked "do you want to come with us?"

"No" Chase replied. "I've noticed that some of the guys are hurting. I think that I will hang around here to see if I can help some of them."

I left to play golf and I had a fun afternoon. But I have not forgotten what Chase did. I spent my afternoon having fun for myself, but he devoted his time to serving others at the Retreat.

Ministry gives. It doesn't take. Here is a test for your ministry: Is it a personal loss or is it a personal gain? True ministry means something is required from you, not that something is acquired by you. Nehemiah understood this fact. He did not take from the people. He served 150 people at his table, plus visiting officials. Neh. 5:17. But he didn't use the governor's food allowance for this service. He did it from his own pocket.

Paul understood this principle. "For you yourselves know how you ought to follow our example, because we did not act in an undisciplined manner among you, nor did we eat anyone's bread without paying for it, but with labor and hardship we kept working night and day so that we might not be a burden to any of you; not because we do not have the right to this, but in order to offer ourselves as a model for you, that you might follow our example." II Thes. 3:7-9. Paul worked as a tentmaker so he could proclaim the gospel through giving, not taking. He had a right to demand support. But he knew his proclamation would be more effective if it did not burden those whom he was serving.

PRINCIPLE: Ministry gives. It doesn't take.

C. WORK OF MINISTRY

The third key to Nehemiah's leadership was his participation in the work. "And I also applied myself to the work on this wall; and we did not buy any land, and all my servants were gathered there for the work." Neh. 5:16.

As governor, Nehemiah had the right to stay behind the scenes. He could have directed the work from the governor's residence as his servants ministered to his personal wants and needs. Instead, Nehemiah positioned himself on the "front lines" and faced the enemy. He participated in the work of ministry himself. The work was that important to him. Here are some benefits of leadership participation in the work:

1. <u>Information.</u> By participating in the work in a community himself, the leader gathers firsthand information about it. This information includes the state of the community and its needs, the people involved, and changes that may be desirable.

2. <u>Connection.</u> Working with other ministers in the community allows the leader to maintain a personal connection with them and with the people of the community. The leader understands the needs, fears, talents and function of the ministers.
3. <u>Training.</u> It is hard to impart what you have not experienced. A leader who is active in the work has standing and experience from which to train others to do the work.
4. <u>Example.</u> A leader who operates on the "front lines" in the community rather than from the back desk sets an example for his whole team, and inspires the team to follow his example in doing the ministry. Perhaps the most important aspect of a leader doing ministry work himself is the expectation it conveys to his people. If the leader is doing the work of the ministry alongside his people, it supports his communicated expectation that the people should be doing the work of the ministry as well as him.

> PRINCIPLE: A leader participates in the work of the ministry alongside his coworkers.

THE TEST

I spoke one time with one of the leading pastors in our city. This man was the senior pastor of a church with thousands of members. We discussed our personal lives and then his church.

At one point the pastor paused. He said "I've got [over 5,000] members in my congregation, and yet I can't seem to get any of them to do any ministry!"

What is the test of effective leadership? The test of effective leadership is productive fruit. Do you recall my discussion with the young pastor about his congregation and its fruitfulness in the Foreword in this book?

Just as fruitfulness is a test of maturity, the test of kingdom leadership is development of abiding, fertile fruit. A "king" produces sterility. He conveys the expectation to his people that he is the Minister. And his people are only too happy to accept this expectation because it is easy for them. They sit in the pew and allow the "king" to do the ministry for them. The people become sterile. This is the spirit of Saul.

An effective leader makes disciples who in turn independently reproduce. If you are an effective leader, you can point to your fruit, just as Nehemiah did. You will be able to point to numerous people that you have helped become fruitful disciples in the kingdom. After twelve years as governor in Jerusalem, Nehemiah could say to the Lord "Remember me, O my God, for good, according to all that I have done for this people." Neh. 5:19.

MEDITATION: "But if He [God] should say thus, 'I have no delight in you,' behold here I am, let Him do to me as seems good to Him." II Sam. 15:26.

1. David said this when he was fleeing Jerusalem as Absalom attempted to seize his throne. In the midst of this power struggle, how important was power to David?

2. How important to David was his personal glory?

3. What was important to David?

4. Why is Jesus called the "son of David"? Mt. 22:42

REVIEW:

1. Dominating leadership is worldly leadership.

2. Nehemiah did not lord his authority over the people of Jerusalem.

    -An effective minister understands his own gifts AND his own limitations.

    -An effective minister regards others as more important than himself.

3. Instead of using his authority to benefit himself, Nehemiah used it to serve the people around him.

    -The purpose of ministry is to serve people.

    -Ministry gives. It doesn't take.

4. Nehemiah participated in the work of ministry himself.

    -A leader participates in the work of the ministry alongside his coworkers.

5. The test of effective leadership is productive fruit.

RESOURCE #3: **CORE VALUES**
("This is our DNA.")

1. Love is the foundation of our ministry.

Explanation: We love God, and we love our fellow man.

2. We work in teams.

Explanation: God's people need help and accountability from one another.

3. Our leadership is a team.

Explanation: Multiple gifts in submission to one another reflect mature ministry.

4. We go minister in the place of need.

Explanation: God calls His people to go to the unsaved and to minister in their world.

5. Our ministry is based on relationship.

Explanation: When you care about a person, you do not abandon him.

6. We meet the needs of the whole person.

Explanation: We share the gospel unto salvation and restore the poor and needy.

7. Every disciple is called to ministry.

Explanation: We equip every disciple in his call and release him into ministry.

8. Each disciple bears fruit.

Explanation: We make disciples who make disciples.

9. Our ministry brings reconciliation.

Explanation: We reconcile people to God and different ethnicities to one another in love and truth.

10. God's glory is paramount.

Explanation: We worship God alone and not one another.

(Core Values were developed by the author and David Garrett, Founder of One7 Ministries.)

RESOURCE #4 – A MINISTRY FRAMEWORK

1. <u>Surround and cover all that you do with prayer.</u>

   Prayer is the basis for everything that we do. Enlist persons who are strong in prayer to pray for the ministry every step of the way. Cover each minister and the territory in which the ministry works in prayer. Use prayer walking as a tool to survey the area and to connect to the people in the area.

2. <u>Church involvement.</u>

   Connect with a local church or body either as a ministry arm of that church or as a defined ministry partner of that church. A church can assist with input, direction, and logistics. A church is a great resource for volunteers, funds, and tools for ministry. Most churches have outreach-minded members that are willing to work if you provide an outlet or structure of ministry for them. You also need to invite persons you meet to a welcoming church body.

3. <u>Explore what is happening in the community.</u>

   This inquiry is a part of the survey of the community. Look at the needs of the community and its people. Ask and see if there are Christians or other ministries already working in the community. There is no need to "reinvent the wheel" if a foundation for ministry has already been laid by other disciples. Build on existing relationships. Use the needs of the community for planning strategies to reach and serve the community.

4. <u>Connect with people in the community.</u>

   Establishing a connection point is the first step in completing the cycle of discipleship. See <u>THE CALL (Book Two – Foundational)</u>. For us, an impetus for moving into a new community has been the realization that existing families with whom we have a relationship moved into that new community, or because participants brought friends from other communities ("Friends bring friends."). We practice sensitivity as to how the Lord is working and moving. Seek the Lord about ways in which you can connect to people of the community, particularly the leaders in the community.

5. <u>Gather people with similar vision and mission.</u>

    Effective ministry is performed in the context of a ministry team. I am amazed at how the Lord connects a diverse group of people and forms a team of ministers. Always look for disciples that might be interested in ministry to a community. Communicate vision for the community to them, and see if the Lord might be calling them to join in the work.

6. <u>Establish presence in the community (Location).</u>

    Presence is the means of influence. Light shines in darkness, so go where they are. We try to spend as much time as possible with the people of the community. We look for an apartment or a house in the community to use as a ministry base. Hold ministry events there, or even better, live there as part of the community itself.

7. <u>Identify leaders (and potential leaders) in the community.</u>

    We always look for disciples within the community. Connect and share the Lord. When you find persons interested in a deeper walk with the Lord, latch onto those persons. Help them to grow in the Lord and to grow in ministry. Disciple, grow and train them in the Lord, even if it takes years. We encourage culturally indigenous ministry because those leaders have huge potential for impact.

8. <u>Partner with other ministries.</u>

    Other ministries are valuable for encouragement, support, ideas, and resource. They also may help in specific areas of need, or assist in an event. We conduct a monthly "Outreach Leaders' Lunch" to bring multiple ministry leaders together for this purpose. Try to establish a mutual connection point.

9. <u>Embrace change as an inevitable dynamic of ministry.</u>

    As the ministry grows and develops, continue to seek vision and guidance for the ministry. Try to anticipate needs and make changes to meet them as they arise. Use sound organization to support healthy organic ministry.

10. <u>Release leaders into ministry.</u>

Be careful to allow new leaders to grow. Make room for them and assist them in identifying and fulfilling the call of God on their lives. If they succeed, then you succeed, especially if they go further than you did. Then, at the right time, release them. Let them go. The success and self-sufficiency of the next generation is important. Leaders should be allowed to lead when they are ready.

LESSON SIXTEEN – THE PALM OF HIS HAND

The Book of Revelation contains some horrifying scenes – earthquakes, famines, plagues, hailstones, wars, massacres, persecutions, murders, panic and death. The book describes a cosmic cataclysmic catastrophe. But at the climax of terror, when the forces of evil are overpowering and all hope seems forsaken, a rider appears.

"And I saw heaven opened, and behold, a white horse, and He who sat on it is called **Faithful and True**, and in righteousness He judges and wages war." Rev. 19:11

Faithful and True. The Book of Nehemiah is a testimony to the faithfulness of God. Against all odds, the wall was built because the Lord is faithful. Badly outnumbered by bitter enemies, the wall was built because the Lord is faithful. Short of resources and burdened with reproach, the wall was built because the Lord is faithful.

Nehemiah trusted God that God would fulfill His word and complete His ordained work if God's people would fear Him and obey His commands. As the wall neared completion, Nehemiah still faced stiff challenges. But Nehemiah's trust in God rather than in his own ability, and safeguards which he established through obedience, enabled him to overcome those challenges.

DISTRACTION

Last weekend, we visited my in-laws in the mountains. I came out of the house and sat on the front porch with my daughters. Cars were stopped in the street beyond the front yard. People had climbed out of their vehicles. They were chasing a herd of cows in the road. The gate in the pasture across the road was askew. The cows were loose. My daughters and I ran to help.

The cows ran right and left as we tried to shoo them back into the pasture. Eventually, we formed a semi-circle large enough to contain the herd, and slowly tightened the circle until the cows went through the gate and back into the pasture. We closed the gate. My father-in-law refastened the chain that locked the entry side of the gate. He grabbed a rope and tied it around that end as well. Confident that the gate was secure, he then set off to search for an even stronger strap to use.

I returned to the front porch and sat with my daughters. As I watched the gate across the road, I noticed that the herd began to regather near it. Then a black and white cow walked up to the gate. She turned her head sideways and stuck it through the bars in the gate. Strange! Next the cow swiveled her head back upright and begin to lift on the gate with her neck! The entry side of the gate with the chain and rope held fast. But the cow lifted the gate off of its hinges on the other side! The cow moved forward and pushed the gate open. The herd could get out again.

I jumped out of my chair on the porch and began running toward the gate – yelling and waving my arms all the while. The cows stopped in their tracks and looked at me as I ran toward them. As I neared the road, a few calves turned and skittered back toward the pasture. Then all the cows turned and ran away as well...except one. As I approached the gate, a black cow just stood there like a wall motionless. Still yelling and gesturing, I got about 10 feet away from the opening when I realized something: It wasn't a cow.

I was face to face with a large black bull.

"Now it came about when it was reported to Sanballat, Tobiah, to Geshem the Arab, and to the rest of our enemies that I had rebuilt the wall, and that no breach remained in it although at that time I had not set up the doors in the gates, that Sanballat and Geshem sent a message to me, saying..." Neh. 6:1-2a.

The wall was built, but Jerusalem was still vulnerable because the doors had not been installed in its gates. Nehemiah's enemies had tried disdain, discouragement, conspiracy and threats to stop the work. Now they resorted to subterfuge.

First, the leaders of surrounding peoples invited Nehemiah to attend a conference outside of Jerusalem. "Come, let us meet together at Chephirim in the plain of Ono." Neh. 6:2b. This invitation made sense in light of Nehemiah's position. He was the governor. It was appropriate for Nehemiah to meet with the leaders of other regions in a summit.

This invitation was intended to appeal to Nehemiah's vanity. "You are the leader in Jerusalem. We are leaders of the surrounding peoples. Let's have a high level conference. It will make us look good and it will make you look good."

But Nehemiah planned the work strategically. Because he knew the critical path to achieve his goals, Nehemiah focused on building the wall and on the activities that were productive in that building. The proposed "summit" would be a distraction from the work which would only cause harm to it and to him. Nehemiah responded, "Why should the work stop while I leave it and come down to you?" Neh. 6:3.

It is important to perform work strategically. Discern between activities that contribute to the goals and activities that are distractions from the goals. Many activities are "good" but actually waste precious time, energy and resources. These good activities may actually hurt the work. Discernment of goals, and the strategic methods which will achieve those goals, protect the integrity of the work.

> Safeguard #1: Avoid distractions. Focus on the strategic plan, its goals and its methods.

Please note that people can also be a distraction. If coworkers have a different vision than your vision, or engage in ministry that does not contribute to the work, they may hinder the work rather than help it. In those situations, the energy and time used to address personnel issues is draining. Some people are life giving coworkers and other people wear you out.

The invitation to summit did not just come one time. Nehemiah's enemies sent the message four times. And four times Nehemiah gave the same, firm answer: "No." Neh. 6:4.

SUBVERSION

The fifth message included an open letter to the king: "It is reported that you want to rebel. You want to be king of Judah!" Neh. 6:5-7. It was a public relations campaign intended for the ears of the people and the ears of the king in Babylon!

This same tactic had worked before when Zerubbabel was rebuilding the temple. Ezra 4:8. At that time, the enemies of Jerusalem sent King Artaxerxes a letter that claimed the Jews were planning to rebel. The King decreed that the work halt. The work on the temple ceased for many years because of that letter.

But this time Nehemiah's example of humble leadership defeated this tactic. The people of Jerusalem knew that Nehemiah did not intend to be king. He didn't behave like an earthly king. Nehemiah used his authority to serve the people, not to dominate them. The people didn't believe the allegations in the letter.

And what about the king of Babylon? The palace knew Nehemiah well. Nehemiah had served the king as cupbearer. The king knew that Nehemiah was not politically ambitious. Nehemiah had served the king humbly, and even waited for the king to initiate the conversation about Jerusalem! Neh. 2:2.

The enemy's tactic failed because of Nehemiah's known character.

> Safeguard #2: Christlike character thwarts the smears of the enemy.

TRUST

Then the enemies employ a false prophet in Jerusalem, Shemaiah, to panic Nehemiah. Shemaiah told Nehemiah "Let us meet together in the house of God, within the temple, and let us close the doors of the temple, for they are coming to kill you, and they are coming to kill you at night." Neh. 6:10b.

Nehemiah, however, trusted God. Nehemiah did not show fear of men or fear of death. He was confident that the Lord was faithful at all times and in all things. "Should a man like me flee? And could one such as I go into the temple to save his life? I will not go in." Neh. 6:11.

Nehemiah also had discernment from the Holy Spirit about this prophet. "Then I perceived that surely God had not sent him..." Neh. 6:12.

> Safeguard #3: Trust the faithfulness of God at all times and in all circumstances.

When I saw the black bull staring at me through the opening, I had a decision – stand or run. Instinctively, I kept moving forward and waving my arms. The bull looked

hard, then turned and ran back to the pasture - to my great relief.

I helped my father-in-law reset the gate, and then secure it so it could not be lifted off its hinges. My father-in-law kept shaking his head and muttering about cows that break out from the wrong side of a gate.

I returned to my daughters on the front porch. My oldest daughter who has a way with words looked at me, smiled a wry smile and said: "Subversive cow!"

REST

"And it came about that just as it grew dark at the gates of Jerusalem before the Sabbath, I commanded that the doors should be shut and that they should not open them until after the Sabbath. Then I stationed some of my servants at the gates so that no load would enter on the Sabbath day." Neh. 13:19.

God ordained the Sabbath rest. He ordained a Sabbath for His people, their animals, and even their land. Ex. 20:9-11; Lev. 25:3-5. The purpose of the Sabbath rest is to benefit man. Mk. 2:27. We need weekly rest and restoration.

Nehemiah was adamant that the Sabbath be observed. He knew the history of Israel's devastation. Failure to obey the Sabbath was a primary reason for Israel's captivity. "But if you do not listen to Me to keep the Sabbath day holy by not carrying a load and coming in through the gates of Jerusalem on the Sabbath day, then I will kindle a fire in its gates and it will devour the palaces of Jerusalem and not be quenched." Jer. 17:27.

But the Sabbath was more important than just causation. The need for Sabbath rest determined the length of the exile. The exile occurred "to fulfill the word of the Lord by the mouth of Jeremiah, until the land had enjoyed its Sabbaths. All the days of its desolation it kept Sabbath until seventy years were complete." II Chron. 36:21. See also Lev. 26:34-35.

Thus, Nehemiah exhorted the people. "What is this evil thing you are doing, by profaning the Sabbath day? Did not your fathers do the same, so that our God brought on us and on this city all this trouble? Yet you are adding to the wrath on Israel by profaning the Sabbath." Neh. 13:17b-18.

The Sabbath was ordained to restore, to renew, to refresh and to recreate. While we are free in Christ, weekly observance of the Sabbath is beneficial and life giving. God created each of us with bodily systems that require renewal. We have an immune system, nervous system, digestive system, cardiovascular system and endocrine system to name a few. These systems need monitoring and they need rest to function properly and to stay in balance.

If we frequently rest and restore, we can sustain our work for many years. Sustaining our work is important because often the work grows in impact and scope through the years. If we ignore the Sabbath, we risk burn out and loss of our ministry.

Also importantly, observing a Sabbath rest is a way in which we can be like God. God "rested on the seventh day; therefore, the Lord blessed the Sabbath day and made it holy." Ex. 20:11. Sabbath observance is an imitation of Christ.

In addition to a weekly Sabbath, we need vacations. Vacations are extended periods of rest that recharge our batteries and reorient our outlook. A minimum of a week is needed for a restorative vacation. And there should be multiple vacations each year (no less than two).

Finally, a place of refuge is recommended. A refuge is a place of quiet (and hopefully beauty) away from the hustle and bustle of work and everyday life. The setting of the refuge alters our state of mind and resets our frame of reference. The environment of peace and tranquility relaxes us. The occasional visit to the refuge refreshes our mind and our soul.

> Safeguard #4: Trust the goodness of God in ordaining a weekly Sabbath rest for you.

We have already described other safeguards that Nehemiah established that sustained the work. Nehemiah instituted a support system for the protection of the workers. See <u>Lesson Ten – Isolation</u>. Each believer needs ongoing relationships of intimate accountability and consistent support. These relationships prompt our growth and help us survive times of crisis.

> Safeguard #5: Ongoing relationships of accountability and support are essential for sustainability.

Another safeguard is a regular reassessment of both personal and ministry activity. The purpose of the reassessment is to prioritize activities and to institute changes as they are necessary.

Nehemiah reassessed and made changes in the building activity when the enemies of Jerusalem began making threats of attack. See <u>Lesson Thirteen – Change</u>.

Every year between Christmas and New Year, I assess my personal life and my ministry participation. I review the events of the past year and their impact. This review is performed in order to gauge effectiveness and to make needed changes. During the review, some of the areas of operation are reprioritized. I decide to change some areas and to add other areas. An area is added when it increases in importance or relevance. But when I decide to add something, I don't just add it. I follow a personal rule: In order to add an area of ministry, I need to drop an area of ministry. Because my personal activity plate is normally full to overflowing, I don't overload. Dropping an area of ministry reinforces the decision that the new area has become a priority.

> Safeguard #6: Regular reassessment of ministry function renews ministry vitality.

THE PIT

I participated in outreach ministry for over 20 years. I experienced ups and downs, successes and defeats, apparent successes that became defeats, and defeats that actually became successes. God called me to the work and so I worked. Then one day my participation came to a grinding halt. My ministry work stopped.

I fell ill. My body stopped producing energy. I lost significant weight and I suffered excruciating pain. My body lost strength until I could not perform simple functions. Some days I was unable to get out of bed to eat and I was bedridden. The doctors performed batteries of scans and tests seeking an answer. They searched for cancer but did not find it. They referred me to North Carolina's leading diagnostic hospital. But the tests revealed no answer other than the possibility of a crippling, untreatable virus.

Days ran into weeks that ran into months. I seemingly lost everything. I was unable to work, unable to care for myself, and unable to participate in ministry. I lay in bed with my life in the balance. I often imagined that God held me in the palm of His hand. There I lay in the middle of His soft hand…hurt, weak and helpless – dependent on the faithfulness and goodness of God.

But what I experienced during my illness is that many areas of ministry did not stop. The other Boyz Club leaders continued with Boyz Club. Other leaders led the MAI Residency training program. The Monday night Bible study guys still came and visited me. Sports outreach ministry continued all over Charlotte.

The fact that ministry continued is due to the work of other people. I did not do it. But one safeguard had contributed to the sustainability of the ministry. It is what I call generational thinking.

I watched a friend of mine over a number of years. He bought a beautiful piece of land in the mountains and built a spacious home on it. It was a stunning estate. When I talked with that friend, however, he seemed to devote much of his spare time to maintaining that estate. And when he visited the estate, he was working in the yard, working on the house or clearing brush.

I felt the Lord prompting me. "David, invest your time and energy in people, not in possessions. The treasures which are laid up in heaven are the lives of people in my kingdom." I tried to heed this guidance although I fell short at times. A major part of my ministry was training young leaders. As those leaders began ministries, I supported them, advised them, and helped the ministries grow. And those ministries continued when I became ill.

Over the course of many months of illness, I slowly regained strength. I still felt horrible, but after 3 months I had energy to function 2-3 hours each day and no more. After 6 months, I had energy to function 4-5 hours each day. My recovery took over 2 years.

But other leaders continued the ministry. My call did not change and I carefully reentered ministry work. I realized that I was not essential to the ministry although other leaders graciously desired my participation. And those leaders had improved some of the areas of ministry.

One impact of my illness is that I have a deeper awareness of the goodness and faithfulness of the Lord.

Generational thinking understands that the tapestry of the kingdom is woven through time and people. Generational thinking understands that personal participation has a limited duration and that no person is permanently indispensable to the work. As a result, investment is made in the lives of younger generations to insure that the duration of the work is not limited to the mortality of one life. The effectiveness of the work is not limited to the ability of one life. The scope of the work is not limited to the vision revealed to one generation.

> Safeguard #7: Generational thinking cultivates long term sustainability of the ministry.

But generational thinking requires mutual submission. Generational thinking requires adherence to this instruction: "Be subject to one another in the fear of Christ." Eph. 5:21.

MEDITATION: "You gave your good Spirit to instruct them and did not withhold your manna from their mouth and gave them water for their thirst. Forty years you sustained them in the wilderness, and they lacked nothing. Their clothes did not wear out and their feet did not swell." Neh. 9:20-21. (ESV)

1. In this passage, Nehemiah testifies to the faithfulness of God in providing for His people. What testimonies did Nehemiah have about the faithfulness of God?

2. What testimonies do you have in your own life about the faithfulness of God?

3. What safeguards have you established in your own life and ministry to enhance sustainability?

4. Why is more detail devoted to the institution of the Sabbath rest than to any of the other Commandments? Ex. 20:9-11

5. What further safeguards do you need to establish in your life and ministry to encourage sustainability?

REVIEW:
1. Nehemiah's enemies tried the tactic of subversion.
2. Safeguard #1: Avoid distractions. Focus on a strategic plan, its goals and its methods.
3. Safeguard #2: Christlike character thwarts the smears of the enemy.
4. Safeguard #3: Trust the faithfulness of God at all times and in all circumstances.
5. Safeguard #4: Trust the goodness of God in ordaining a weekly Sabbath rest for you.
6. Safeguard #5: Ongoing relationships of accountability and support are essential for sustainability.
7. Safeguard #6: Regular reassessment of ministry function renews ministry vitality.
8. Safeguard #7: Generational thinking cultivates long term sustainability of the ministry.

THE LAST WORD

"So the wall was completed on the twenty-fifth of the month Elul, in fifty-two days." Neh. 6:15

The completion of the wall in Jerusalem did not end Nehemiah's work. He stayed in Jerusalem for twelve more years. Then Nehemiah returned to Babylon for a short period as he had promised the king when he left. Thereafter Nehemiah came back to Jerusalem. Neh. 5:14; 13:6-7.

The first half of the Book of Nehemiah tells of building the wall. The second half tells of what Nehemiah did after the wall was built. Nehemiah's work after completion of the wall can be encapsulated in two words: Body Life. Nehemiah oversaw the presentation of the precepts of God to Jerusalem (Neh. 8), and the people made a covenant to observe them. (Neh. 10). Worship in the temple, giving of the tithe and observation of the Sabbath – these were all restored. (Neh. 12-13). Uncleanness and defilement were banished. Nehemiah emphasized consecration, lifestyle, community and commitment.

Body life is essential to any group of disciples. Worship, fellowship and sacramental celebration are vital, just as consecration, lifestyle, community and commitment should be taught and woven into the fabric of body life.

Yet body life is incomplete without outreach. The body must continually go out and reach out, or it fails in its essential worldly mission. And it fails to be Christ's Body.

The vision for the work is not just in one area. In Nehemiah's day, a wall was built to protect a city. But as the city expanded, so did the wall. Excavations of ancient cities, including Jerusalem, reveal multiple walls – inner walls and outer walls; defensive walls and outposts.

Likewise, the vision for the kingdom of God is not just in one community. God may call a body to work in an area, and that body must work where God calls it. But the work is a territorial progression. It expands into new areas. We began in one neighborhood in Charlotte, and our ministry partners now work in six neighborhoods. The work has expanded to other cities as well.

The work is "Jerusalem, Judea and Samaria, and even to the remotest part of the earth." Acts 1:8. As God reveals his plan, the work progresses and expands into a community, then a city, and then beyond.

Whether it is 52 days or 52 years, the work must progress. And the work continues...until He comes and gathers all unto Himself for an account.

"In that day this song will be sung in the land of Judah:
'We have a strong city;
He sets up walls and ramparts for security.
Open the gates, that the righteous nations may enter,
The one that remains faithful.
The steadfast of mind Thou wilt keep in perfect peace,
Because he trusts in Thee.'" Isa. 26:1-3.

NOTES:

NOTES:

NOTES:

www.ingramcontent.com/pod-product-compliance
Lightning Source LLC
LaVergne TN
LVHW081356060426
835510LV00016B/1871